# Maxims

By

Napoleon Bonaparte

## MAXIM I

The frontiers of states are either large rivers, or chains of mountains, or deserts. Of all these obstacles to the march of an army, the most difficult to overcome is the desert; mountains come next, and broad rivers occupy the third place.

NOTE.

Napoleon, in his military career, appears to have been called upon to surmount every difficulty which can occur in wars of invasion.

In Egypt he traversed deserts, and vanquished and destroyed the Mamelukes, so celebrated for their address and courage. His genius knew how to accommodate itself to all the dangers of this distant enterprise, in a country ill adapted to supply the wants of his troops.

In the conquest of Italy, he twice crossed the Alps by the most difficult passes, and at a season, too, which rendered this undertaking still more formidable. In three months he passed the Pyrenees, defeated and dispersed four Spanish armies. In short, from the Rhine to the Borysthenes, no natural obstacle could be found to arrest the rapid march of his victorious army.

## MAXIM II

In forming the plan of a campaign, it is requisite to foresee everything the enemy may do, and to be prepared with the necessary means to counteract it.

Plans of campaign may be modified ad infinitum according to circumstances—the genius of the general, the character of the troops, and the topography of the theatre of action.

NOTE.

Sometimes we see a hazardous campaign succeed, the plan of which is directly at variance with the principles of the art of war. But this success depends generally on the caprice of fortune, or upon faults committed by the enemy—two things upon which a general must never count. Sometimes the plan of a campaign, although based on sound principles of war, runs the risk of failing at the outset if opposed by an adversary who acts at first on the defensive, and then, suddenly seizing the initiative, surprises by the skilfulness of his manœuvres. Such was the fate of the plan laid down by the Aulic council for the campaign of 1796, under the command of Marshal Wurmser. From his great numerical superiority, the marshal had calculated on the entire destruction of the French army, by cutting off its retreat. He founded his operations on the defensive attitude of his adversary, who was posted on the line of the Adige, and had to cover the siege of Mantua, as well as central and lower Italy.

Wurmser, supposing the French army fixed in the neighborhood of Mantua, divided his forces into three corps, which marched separately, intending to unite at that place. Napoleon, having penetrated the design of the Austrian general, perceived the advantage to be derived from striking the first blow against an army divided into three corps, with no communication between them. He hastened, therefore, to raise the siege of Mantua, assembled the whole of his forces, and by this means became superior to the imperialists, whose divisions he attacked and beat in detail. Thus Wurmser, who fancied he had only to march to certain victory, saw himself compelled, after ten days campaign, to retire with the remains of his army into the Tyrol, after a loss of twenty-five thousand men in killed and wounded, fifteen thousand prisoners, nine stand of colors, and seventy pieces of cannon.

Hence, nothing is so difficult as to prescribe beforehand to a general the line of conduct he shall pursue during the course of a campaign. Success must often depend on circumstances that cannot be foreseen; and it should be remembered, likewise, that nothing cramps so much the efforts of genius as compelling the head of an army to be governed by any will but his own.

## MAXIM III

An army which undertakes the conquest of a country, has its two wings resting either upon neutral territories, or upon great natural obstacles, such as rivers or chains of mountains. It happens in some cases that only one wing is so supported; and in others that both are exposed.

In the first instance cited, viz., where both wings are protected, a general has only to protect his front from being penetrated. In the second, where one wing only is supported, he should rest upon the supported wing. In the third, where both wings are exposed, he should depend upon a central formation, and never allow the different corps under his command to depart from this: for if it be difficult to contend with the disadvantage of having two flanks exposed, the inconvenience is doubled by having four, trebled if there be six— that is to say, if the army is divided into two or three different corps. In the first instance, then, as above quoted, the line of operation may rest indifferently on the right or on the left. In the second, it should be directed toward the wing in support. In the third, it should be perpendicular to the centre of the army's line of march. But in all these cases it is necessary, at a distance of every five or six days march, to have a strong post or an entrenched position upon the line of operation, in order to collect military stores and provisions, to organize convoys, to form of it a centre of movement, and establish a point of defence to shorten the line of operation of the army.

NOTE.

These general principles in the art of war were entirely unknown, or lost sight of, in the middle ages. The crusaders in their incursions into Palestine appear to have had no object but to fight and to conquer, so little pains did they take to profit by their victories. Hence, innumerable armies perished in Syria, without any other advantage than that derived from the momentary success obtained by superior numbers.

It was by the neglect of these principles, also, that Charles XII, abandoning his line of operation and all communication with Sweden, threw himself into the Ukraine, and lost the greater part of his army by the fatigue of a winter campaign in a barren country destitute of resources.

Defeated at Pultawa, he was obliged to seek refuge in Turkey, after crossing the Nieper with the remains of his army, diminished to little more than one thousand men.

Gustavus Adolphus was the first who brought back the art of war to its true principles. His operations in Germany were bold, rapid, and well executed. He made success at all times conducive to future security, and established his line of operation so as to prevent the possibility of any interruption in his communications with Sweden. His campaigns form a new era in the art of war.

## MAXIM IV

When the conquest of a country is undertaken by two or three armies, which have each their separate line of operation, until they arrive at a point fixed upon for their concentration, it should be laid down as a principle, that the union of these different corps should never take place near the enemy; because the enemy, in uniting his forces, may not only prevent this junction, but may beat the armies in detail.

NOTE.

In the campaign of 1757, Frederick, marching to the conquest of Bohemia with two armies, which had each their separate line of operation, succeeded, notwithstanding, in uniting them in sight of the Duke of Lorraine, who covered Prague with the imperial army; but his example should not be followed. The success of this march depended entirely on the inaction of the duke, who, at the head of seventy thousand men, did nothing to prevent the junction of the two Prussian armies.

## MAXIM V

All wars should be governed by certain principles, for every war should have a definite object, and be conducted according to the rules of art. (A war should only be undertaken with forces proportioned to the obstacles to be overcome.)

NOTE.

It was a saying of Marshal Villars, that when war is decided on, it is necessary to have exact information of the number of troops the enemy can bring into the field, since it is impossible to lay down any solid plan of offensive or defensive operation without an accurate knowledge of what you have to expect and fear. "When the first shot is fired," observes Marshal Villars, "no one can calculate what will be the issue of the war. It is, therefore, of vast importance to reflect maturely before we begin it." When once, however, this is decided, the marshal observes that the boldest and most extended plans are generally the wisest and the most successful. "When we are determined upon war," he adds, "we should carry it on vigorously and without trifling."

## MAXIM VI

At the commencement of a campaign, to advance or not to advance, is a matter for grave consideration; but when once the offensive has been assumed, it must be sustained to the last extremity. However skilful the manœuvres in a retreat, it will always weaken the morale of an army, because, in losing the chances of success, these last are transferred to the enemy. Besides, retreats always cost more men and materiel than the most bloody engagements; with this difference, that in a battle the enemy's loss is nearly equal to your own—whereas in a retreat the loss is on your side only.

NOTE.

Marshal Saxe remarks, that no retreats are so favorable as those which are made before a languid and unenterprising enemy, for when he pursues with vigor, the retreat soon degenerates into a rout. "Upon this principle it is a great error," says the marshal, "to adhere to the proverb which recommends us to build a bridge of gold for a retreating enemy. No; follow him up with spirit, and he is destroyed!"

## MAXIM VII

An army should be ready every day, every night, and at all times of the day and night, to oppose all the resistance of which it is capable. With this view, the soldier should always be furnished completely with arms and ammunition; the infantry should never be without its artillery, its cavalry, and its generals; and the different divisions of the army should be constantly in a state to support, to be supported, and to protect itself.

The troops, whether halted, or encamped, or on the march, should be always in favorable positions, possessing the essentials required for a field of battle; for example, the flanks should be well covered, and all the artillery so placed as to have free range, and to play with the greatest advantage. When an army is in column of march, it should have advanced guards and flanking parties, to examine well the country in front, to the right, and to the left, and always at such distance as to enable the main body to deploy into position.

NOTE.

The following maxims, taken from the memoirs of Montécuculli, appear to me well suited to this place, and calculated to form a useful commentary on the general principles laid down in the preceding maxim:

1. When war has been once decided on, the moment is past for doubts and scruples. On the contrary, we are bound to hope that all the evil which may ensue, will not; that Providence, or our own wisdom, may avert it; or that the want of talent on the part of the enemy may prevent him from benefiting by it. The first security for success is to confer the command on one individual. When the authority is divided, the opinions of the commanders often vary, and the operations are deprived of that ensemble which is the first essential to victory. Besides, when an enterprise is common to many, and not confined to a single person, it is conducted without vigor, and less interest is attached to the result.

After having strictly conformed to all the rules of war, and satisfied ourselves that nothing has been omitted to ensure eventual success, we must then leave the issue in the hands of Providence, and repose ourselves tranquilly in the decision of a higher power.

Let what will arrive, it is the part of a general-in-chief to remain firm and constant in his purposes; he must not allow himself to be elated by prosperity, nor to be depressed by adversity: for in war good and bad and fortune succeed each other by turns, form the ebb and flow of military operations.

2. When your own army is strong and inured to service, and that of the enemy is weak and consists of new levies, or of troops enervated by long inaction, then you should exert every means to bring him to battle.

If, on the other hand, your adversary has the advantage in troops, a decisive combat is to be avoided, and you must be content to impede his progress, by encamping advantageously, and fortifying favorable passes. When armies are nearly equal in force, it is desirable not to avoid a battle, but only to attempt to fight one to advantage. For this purpose, care should be taken to encamp always in front of the enemy; to move when he moves, and occupy the heights and advantageous grounds that lie upon his line of march; to seize upon all the buildings and roads adjoining to his camp, and post yourself advantageously in the places by which he must pass. It is always something gained to make him lose time, to thwart his designs, or to retard their progress and execution. If, however, an army is altogether inferior to that of the enemy, and there is no possibility of manœuvring against him with success, then the campaign must be abandoned, and the troops must retire into the fortresses.

3. The principal object of a general-in-chief, in the moment of battle, should be to secure the flanks of his army. It is true that natural positions may be found to effect this object, but these positions being fixed and immovable in themselves, they are only advantageous to a general who wishes to wait the shock of the enemy, and not to one who marches to the attack.

A general can, therefore, rely only on the proper arrangement of his troops, to enable him to repel any attempt the adversary may make upon the front, or flanks, or rear of his army.

If one flank of an army rests upon a river, or an impassable ravine, the whole of the cavalry may be posted with the other wing, in order to envelop the enemy more easily by its superiority in numbers.

If the enemy has his flanks supported by woods, light cavalry or infantry should be despatched to attack him in flank or in rear during the heat of the battle. If practicable, also, an attack should be made upon the baggage, to add to his confusion.

If you desire to beat the enemy's left with your right wing, or his right with your left wing, the wing with which you attack should be reinforced by the élite of your army. At the same moment, the other wing should avoid battle, and the attacking wing brought rapidly forward, so as to overwhelm the enemy. If the nature of the ground admits, he should be approached by stealth, and attacked before he is on his guard. If any signs of fear are discoverable in the enemy, and which are always to be detected by confusion or disorder in his movements, he should be pursued immediately, without allowing him time to recover himself. It is now the cavalry should be brought into action, and manœuvre so as to surprise and cut off his artillery and baggage.

4. The order of march should always be subservient to the order of battle, which last should be arranged beforehand. The march of an army is always well regulated when it is governed by the distance to be accomplished, and by the time required for its performance. The front of the column of march should be diminished or increased according to the nature of the country, taking care that the artillery always proceeds by the main road.

When a river is to be passed, the artillery should be placed in battery upon the bank opposite the point of crossing.

It is a great advantage, when a river forms a sweep or angle, and when a ford is to be found near the place where you wish to effect a passage. As the construction of the bridge proceeds, infantry should be advanced to cover the workmen, by keeping up a fire on the opposite bank; but the moment it is finished, a corps of infantry and cavalry, and some field-pieces, should be pushed across. The infantry should entrench itself immediately at the head of the bridge, and it is prudent, moreover, to fortify on the same side of the river, in order to protect the bridge in case the enemy should venture an offensive movement.

The advanced guard of an army should be always provided with trusty guides, and with a corps of pioneers: the first to point out the best roads, the second to render these roads more practicable.

If the army marches in detachments, the commander of each detachment should be furnished with the name of the place in writing, where the whole are to be reassembled; the place should be sufficiently removed from the enemy to prevent him from occupying it before the junction of all the detachments. To this end, it is of importance to keep the name a secret.

From the moment an army approaches the enemy, it should march in the order in which it is intended to fight. If anything is to be apprehended, precautions are necessary in proportion to the degree of the danger. When a defile is to be passed, the troops should be halted beyond the extremity, until the whole army has quitted the defile.

In order to conceal the movements of an army, it is necessary to march by night through woods and valleys, by the most retired roads, and out of reach of all inhabited places. No fires should be allowed; and, to favor the design still more, the troops should move by verbal order. When the object of the march is to carry a post, or to relieve a place that is besieged, the advanced guard should march within musket shot of the main body, because then you are prepared for an immediate attack, and ready to overthrow all before you.

When a march is made to force a pass guarded by the enemy, it is desirable to make a feint upon one point, while, by a rapid movement, you bring your real attack to bear upon another.

Sometimes success is obtained by pretending to fall back upon the original line of march, and, by a sudden countermarch, seizing upon the pass, before the enemy is able to reoccupy it. Some generals have gained their point by manœuvring so as to deceive the enemy, while a detachment under the cover of high grounds has surprised the passage by a stolen march. The enemy being engaged in watching the movements of the main body, the detachment has an opportunity of entrenching itself in its new position.

5. An army regulates its mode of encampment according to the greater or less degree of precaution, when circumstances require. In a friendly country the troops are divided, to afford better accommodation and supplies. But with the enemy in front, an army should always encamp in order of battle. With this view, it is of the highest importance to cover one part of the camp, as far as practicable, by natural defences, such as a river, a chain of rocks, or a ravine. Care should be taken also that the camp is not commanded, and that there is no obstacle to a free communication between the different corps, and which can prevent the troops from mutually succoring each other.

When an army occupies a fixed camp, it is necessary to be well supplied with provisions and ammunition, or at least that these should be within certain reach and easily obtained. To insure this, the line of communication must be well established, and care taken not to leave an enemy's fortress in your rear.

When an army is established in winter quarters, its safety is best secured either by fortifying a camp (for which purpose a spot should be selected near a large commercial town, or a river affording facility of transport), or by distributing it in close cantonments, so that the troops should be near together, and capable of affording each other mutual support.

The winter quarters of an army should be protected, likewise, by constructing small covered works on all the lines of approach to the cantonments, and by posting advanced guards of cavalry to observe the motions of the enemy.

6. A battle is to be sought, when there is reason to hope for victory, or when an army runs the risk of being ruined without fighting; also when a besieged place is to be relieved, or when you desire to prevent a reinforcement from reaching the enemy. Battles are useful, likewise, when we wish to profit by a favorable opportunity which offers, to secure a certain advantage, such as seizing upon an undefended point or pass, attacking the enemy when he has committed a fault, or when some misunderstanding among his generals favors the undertaking.

If an enemy declines an engagement, he may be compelled to it, either by besieging a place of importance, or by falling upon him unawares, and when he cannot easily effect his retreat. Or (after pretending to retire), by making a rapid countermarch, attacking him vigorously and forcing him to action.

The different circumstances under which a battle should be avoided or declined, are, when there is greater danger to be apprehended from defeat than advantage to be derived from victory; when you are very inferior to your adversary in numbers, and are expecting reinforcements; above all, when the enemy is advantageously posted, or when he is contributing to his own ruin by some inherent defect in his position, or by the errors and divisions of his generals.

To gain a battle, each arm must be advantageously posted, and have the means of engaging its front and in flank. The wings must be protected by natural obstacles, where these present themselves, or by having recourse when necessary to the aid of art.

The troops must be able to assist each other without confusion, and care must be taken that the broken corps do not fall back upon, and throw the rest into disorder. Above all, the intervals between the different corps must be sufficiently small to prevent the enemy from penetrating between them, for in that case you would be obliged to employ your reserves, and run the risk of being entirely overwhelmed. Sometimes victory is obtained by creating a diversion in the middle of a battle, or even by depriving the soldier of all hope of retreat, and placing him in a situation where he is reduced to the necessity either to conquer or die.

At the commencement of a battle, if the ground is level, you should advance to meet the enemy, in order to inspire the soldier with courage; but if you are well posted, and your artillery advantageously placed, then wait for him with determination: remembering always to fight resolutely, to succor opportunely those who require it, and never to bring your reserves into action except in the last extremity; and even then to preserve some support, behind which the broken corps may rally.

When it is necessary to attack with your whole force, the battle should commence toward evening; because then, whatever be the issue, night will arrive to separate the combatants before your troops are exhausted. By this means, an opportunity is afforded of affecting an orderly retreat if the result of the battle requires it.

During an action, the general-in-chief should occupy some spot whence he can, as far as possible, overlook his whole army. He should be informed, immediately, of everything that passes in the different divisions. He should be ready, in order to render success more complete, to operate with fresh troops upon those points where the enemy is giving way, and also to reinforce his own corps wherever they are inclined to yield. When the enemy is beaten, he must pursue him instantly, without giving him a moment to rally; on the other hand, if he is himself defeated, or despairs of victory, he must retreat in the best possible order.

7. It shows great talent in a general to bring troops, who are prepared for action, into collision with those who are not: for example, fresh troops against those which are exhausted—brave and disciplined men against recruits. He must likewise be ready always to fall with his army upon a weak or detached corps, to follow the track of the enemy, and charge him among defiles before he can face about and get into position.

8. A position is good when the different corps are so placed as to be engaged with advantage, and without any remaining unemployed. If you are superior in cavalry, positions are to be taken in plains and open ground; if in infantry, in an enclosed and covered country. If inferior in numbers, in confined and narrow places; if superior, in a spacious and extensive field. With a very inferior army, a difficult pass must be selected to occupy and fortify.

9. In order to obtain every possible advantage from a diversion, we should ascertain first, that the country in which it is to be created is easily penetrated. A diversion should be made vigorously, and on those points where it is calculated to do the greatest mischief to the enemy.

10. To make war with success, the following principles should never be departed from:

To be superior to your enemy in numbers, as well as in morale; to fight battles in order to spread terror in the country; to divide your army into as many corps as may be effected without risk, in order to undertake several objects at the same time; to treat WELL those who yield, to ILL treat those who resist; to secure your rear, and occupy and strengthen yourself at the outset in some post which shall serve as a central point for the support of your future movements; to guard against desertion; to make yourself master of the great rivers and principal passes, and to establish your line of communication by getting possession of the fortresses, by laying siege to them, and of the open country, by giving battle; for it is vain to expect that conquests are to be achieved without combats; although when a victory is won, they will be best maintained by uniting mildness with valor.

## MAXIM VIII

A general-in-chief should ask himself frequently in the day: "What should I do if the enemy's army appeared now in my front, or on my right, or my left?" If he have any difficulty in answering these questions, his position is bad, and he should seek to remedy it.

NOTE.

In the campaign of 1758, the position of the Prussian army at Hohen Kirk, being commanded by the batteries of the enemy, who occupied all the heights, was eminently defective; notwithstanding, Frederick, who saw his rear menaced by the corps of Laudon, remained six days in his camp without seeking to correct his position. It would seem, indeed, that he was ignorant of his real danger: for Marshal Daun, having manœuvred during the night in order to attack by daybreak, surprised the Prussians in their lines before they were able to defend themselves, and by this means surrounded them completely.

Frederick succeeded, however, in effecting his retreat with regularity, but not without the loss of ten thousand men, many general officers, and almost all of his artillery. If Marshal Daun had followed up his victory with greater boldness, the king of Prussia would never have been able to rally his army. On this occasion, Frederick's good fortune balanced his imprudence.

Marshal Saxe remarks, that there is more talent than is dreamt of in bad dispositions, if we possess the art of converting them into good ones when the favorable moment arrives. Nothing astonishes the enemy so much as this manœuvre; he has counted upon something; all his arrangements have been founded upon it accordingly—and at the moment of attack it escapes him! "I must repeat," says the marshal, "there is nothing that so completely disconcerts an enemy as this, or leads him to commit so many errors; for it follows, that if he does not change his arrangements, he is beaten; and if he does change them, in presence of his adversary, he is equally undone."

It seems to me, however, that a general who should rest the success of a battle upon such a principle, would be more likely to lose than to gain by it; for if he had to deal with a skilful adversary and an alert tactician, the latter would find time to take advantage of the previous bad arrangements, before he would be able to remedy them.


## MAXIM IX

The strength of an army, like the power in mechanics, is estimated by multiplying the mass by the rapidity; a rapid march augments the morale of an army, and increases its means of victory. Press on!

NOTE.

"Rapidity," says Montécuculli, "is of importance in concealing the movements of an army, because it leaves no time to divulge the intention of its chief. It is, therefore, an advantage to attack the enemy unexpectedly, to take him off his guard, to surprise him, and let him feel the thunder before he sees the flash; but if too great celerity exhausts your troops, while, on the other hand, delay deprives you of the favorable moment, you must weigh the advantage against the disadvantage, and choose between."

Marshal Villars observes, that "in war everything depends upon being able to deceive the enemy; and having once gained this point, in never allowing him time to recover himself." Villars has united practice to precept. His bold and rapid marches were almost always crowned with success.

It was the opinion of Frederick that all wars should be short and rapid; because a long war insensibly relaxes discipline, depopulates the state, and exhausts its resources.


## MAXIM X

When an army is inferior in number, inferior in cavalry, and in artillery, it is essential to avoid a general action. The first deficiency should be supplied by rapidity of movement; the want of artillery, by the nature of the manœuvres; and the inferiority in cavalry, by the choice of positions. In such circumstances, the morale of the soldier does much.

NOTE.

The campaign of 1814 in France was skilfully executed upon these principles. Napoleon, with an army inferior in number, an army discouraged by the disastrous retreats of Moscow and of Leipzig, and still more by the presence of the enemy in the French territory, contrived, notwithstanding, to supply his vast inequality of force by the rapidity and combination of his movements. By the success obtained at Champ-Aubert, Montmirail, Montereau, and Rheims, he began to restore the morale of the French army. The numerous recruits of which it was composed, had already acquired that steadiness of which the old regiments afforded them an example, when the capture of Paris, and the astonishing revolution it produced, compelled Napoleon to lay down his arms.

But this consequence resulted rather from the force of circumstances than from any absolute necessity; for Napoleon, by carrying his army to the other side of the Loire, might easily have formed a junction with the armies of the Alps and Pyrenees, and have reappeared on the field of battle at the head of a hundred thousand men. Such a force would have amply sufficed to re-establish the chances of war in his favor; more especially as the armies of the allied sovereigns were obliged to manœuvre upon the French territory with all the strong places of Italy and France in their rear.

## MAXIM XI

To direct operations with lines far removed from each other, and without communications, is to commit a fault which always gives birth to a second. The detached column has only its orders for the first day. Its operations on the following day depend upon what may have happened to the main body. Thus, this column either loses time upon emergency, in waiting for orders, or it will act without them, and at hazard. Let it therefore be held as a principle, that an army should always keep its columns so united as to prevent the enemy from passing between them with impunity. Whenever, for particular reasons, this principle is departed from, the detached corps should be independent in their operations. They should move toward a point fixed upon for their future junction. They should advance without hesitating, and without waiting for fresh orders; and every precaution should be taken to prevent an attack upon them in detail.

NOTE.

The Austrian army, commanded by Field-marshal Alvinzi, was divided into two corps, destined to act independently, until they should accomplish their junction before Mantua. The first of these corps, consisting of forty-five thousand men, was under the orders of Alvinzi. It was to debouch by Monte Baldo, upon the positions occupied by the French army on the Adige. The second corps, commanded by General Provéra, was destined to act upon the lower Adige, and to raise the blockade of Mantua. Napoleon, informed of the enemy's movements, but not entirely comprehending his projects, confined himself to concentrating his masses, and giving orders to the troops to hold themselves in readiness to manœuvre. In the meantime, fresh information satisfied the general-in-chief of the French army that the corps which had debouched by La Coronna, over Monte Baldo, was endeavoring to form a junction with its cavalry and artillery—both which, having crossed the Adige at Dolce, were directing their march upon the plateau of Rivoli, by the great road leading by Incanole.

Napoleon immediately foresaw that, by having possession of the plateau, he should be able to prevent this junction, and obtain all the advantages of the initiative. He accordingly put his troops in motion, and at two o'clock in the morning occupied that important position. Once master of the point fixed upon for the junction of the Austrian columns, success followed all his dispositions. He repulsed every attack, made seven thousand prisoners, and took several standards and twelve pieces of cannon. At two o'clock in the afternoon, the battle of Rivoli was already gained, when Napoleon, learning that General Provéra had passed the Adige at Anghiari, and was directing his march upon Mantua, left to his generals the charge of following up the retreat of Alvinzi, and placed himself at the head of a division for the purpose of defeating the designs of Provéra.

By a rapid march, he again succeeded in the initiatory movement, and in preventing the garrison of Mantua from uniting its force with the relieving army. The corps intrusted with the blockade, eager to distinguish itself under the eyes of the conqueror of Rivoli, compelled the garrison to retire into the place, while the division of Victor, forgetting the fatigues of a forced march, rushed with impetuosity on the relieving army in front. At this moment a sortie from the lines of St. George took him in flank, while the corps of Augereau, which had followed the march of the Austrian general, attacked him in rear. Provéra, surrounded on all sides, capitulated. The result of these two battles cost the Austrians three thousand men in killed and wounded, twenty-two thousand prisoners, twenty-four standards, and forty-six pieces of cannon.

### MAXIM XII

An army ought to have only one line of operation. This should be preserved with care, and never abandoned but in the last extremity.

NOTE.

"The line of communication of an army," says Montécuculli, "must be certain and well established, for every army that acts from a distant base, and is not careful to keep this line perfectly open, marches upon a precipice. It moves to certain ruin, as may be seen by an infinity of examples. In fact, if the road by which provisions, ammunition and reinforcements are to be brought up, is not entirely secured—if the magazines, the hospitals, the depôts of arms, and the places of supply are not fixed and commodiously situated—not only the army cannot keep the field, but it will be exposed to the greatest dangers."

## MAXIM XIII

The distances permitted between corps of an army upon the march must be governed by the localities, by circumstances, and by the object in view.

NOTE.

When an army moves at a distance from the enemy, the columns may be disposed along the road so as to favor the artillery and baggage. But when it is marching into action, the different corps must be formed in close columns in order of battle. The generals must take care that the heads of the columns, which are to attack together, do not outstep each other, and that in approaching the field of action they preserve the relative intervals required for deployment.

"The marches that are made preparatory to a battle require," says Frederick, "the greatest precaution." With this view, he recommends his generals to be particularly on their guard, and to reconnoitre the ground at successive distances, in order to secure the initiative by occupying those positions most calculated to favor an attack. On a retreat, it is the opinion of many generals that an army should concentrate its forces, and march in close columns if it is still strong enough to resume the offensive; for by this means it is easy to form the line when a favorable opportunity presents itself, either for holding the enemy in check or for attacking him if he is not in a situation to accept battle.

Such was Moreau's retreat after the passage of the Adda by the Austro-Russian army. The French general, after having covered the evacuation of Milan, took up a position between the Po and the Tanaro.

His camp rested upon Alexandria and Valentia, two capital fortresses, and had the advantage of covering the roads to Turin and Savona, by which he could effect his retreat in case he was unable to accomplish a junction with the corps d'armee of Macdonald, who had been ordered to quit the kingdom of Naples, and hasten his march into Tuscany.

Forced to abandon his position in consequence of the insurrection in

Piedmont and Tuscany, Moreau retired upon Asti, where he learned that his communication with the river of Genoa had just been cut off by the capture of Ceva. After several ineffectual attempts to retake this place, he saw that his only safety depended upon throwing himself into the mountains.

To effect this object, he directed the whole of his battering train and heavy baggage by the Col de Fenestrelle upon France; then opening himself a way over the St. Bernard, he gained Loano with his light artillery and the small proportion of field equipment he had been able to preserve.

By this skilful movement, he not only retained his communications with France, but was enabled to observe the motions of the army from Naples, and to facilitate his junction with it by directing the whole of his force upon the points necessary for that purpose.

Macdonald, in the meantime, whose only chance of success depended on concentrating his little army, neglected this precaution, and was beaten in three successive actions at the Trebia.

By this retardment of his march, he rendered all Moreau's measures to unite the two armies in the plains of the Po useless, and his retreat, after his brilliant but fruitless efforts at the Trebia, defeated the other arrangements, also, which the former had made to come to his support. The inactivity of Marshal Suwarrow, however, finally enabled the French general to accomplish his junction with the remains of the army from Naples. Moreau then concentrated his whole force upon the Appenines, and placed himself in a situation to defend the important positions of Liguria, until the chances of war should afford him an opportunity of resuming the offensive.

When, after a decisive battle, an army has lost its artillery and equipments, and is consequently no longer in a state to assume the offensive, or even to arrest the pursuit of the enemy, it would seem most desirable to divide what remains into several corps, and order them to march by separate and distant routes upon the base of operation, and throw themselves into the fortresses. This is the only means of safety: for the enemy, uncertain as to the precise direction taken by the vanquished army, is ignorant in the first instance which corps to pursue, and it is in this moment of indecision that a march is gained upon him. Besides, the movements of a small body being so much easier than those of a larger one, these separate lines of march are all in favor of a retreating army.

## MAXIM XIV

Among mountains, a great number of positions are always to be found very strong in themselves, and which it is dangerous to attack. The character of this mode of warfare consists in occupying camps on the flanks or in the rear of the enemy, leaving him only the alternative of abandoning his position without fighting, to take up another in the rear, or to descend from it in order to attack you. In mountain warfare, the assailant has always the disadvantage; even in offensive warfare in the open field, the great secret consists in defensive combats, and in obliging the enemy to attack.

NOTE.

During the campaign of 1793, in the Maritime Alps, the French army, under the orders of General Brunet, did all in its power to get possession of the camps at Raus and at Fourches, by an attack in front. But these useless efforts served only to increase the courage of the Piedmontese, and to destroy the élite of the grenadiers of the republican army. The manœuvres by which Napoleon, without fighting, compelled the enemy to evacuate these positions in 1796, suffice to establish the truth of these principles, and to prove how much success in war depends upon the genius of the general as well as on the courage of the soldier.


## MAXIM XV


The first consideration with a general who offers battle, should be the glory and honor of his arms; the safety and preservation of his men is only the second; but it is in the enterprise and courage resulting from the former, that the latter will most assuredly be found. In a retreat, besides the honor of the army, the loss of life is often greater than in two battles. For this reason, we should never despair while brave men are to be found with their colors. It is by this means that we obtain victory, and deserve to obtain it.

NOTE.

In 1645, the French army, under the orders of the Prince of Condé, was on the march to lay siege to Nordlingen, when it was discovered that Count Merci, who commanded the Bavarians, had foreseen this intention, and had entrenched himself in a strong position which defended Nordlingen at the same time that it covered Donawerth.

Notwithstanding the favorable position of the enemy, Condé ordered the attack. The combat was terrible. All the infantry in the centre and on the right, after being successively engaged, was routed and dispersed, in spite of the efforts of the cavalry and the reserve, which were likewise carried away with the fugitives. The battle was lost. Condé, in despair, having no longer either centre or right to depend upon, collected the remnants of his battalions, and directed his march to the left, where Turenne was still engaged. This perseverance reanimated the ardor of the troops. They broke the right wing of the enemy, and Turenne, by a change of front, returned to the attack upon his centre. Night, too, favored the boldness of Condé. An entire corps of Bavarians, fancying themselves cut off, laid down their arms; and the obstinacy of the French general in this struggle for victory was repaid by possession of the field of battle, together with a great number of prisoners, and almost all the enemy's artillery. The Bavarian army beat a retreat, and the next day Nordlingen capitulated.

## MAXIM XVI

It is an approved maxim in war, never to do what the enemy wishes you to do, for this reason alone, that he desires it. A field of battle, therefore, which he has previously studied and reconnoitred, should be avoided, and double care should be taken where he has had time to fortify and entrench. One consequence deducible from this principle is, never to attack a position in front which you can gain by turning.

NOTE.

It was without due regard to this principle, that Marshal Villeroi, on assuming the command of the army of Italy, during the campaign of 1701, attacked, with unwarrantable presumption, Prince Eugene, of Savoy, in his entrenched position of Chiavi, on the Oglio. The French generals, Catinat among the rest, considered the post unassailable, but Villeroi insisted, and the result of this otherwise unimportant battle was the loss of the élite of the French army. It would have been greater still, but for Catinat's exertions.

It was by neglecting the same principle, that the Prince of Condé, in the campaign of 1644, failed in all his attacks upon the entrenched position of the Bavarian army. The Count Merci, who commanded the latter, had drawn up his cavalry skilfully upon the plain, resting upon Freyberg, while his infantry occupied the mountain. After many fruitless attempts, the Prince of Condé, seeing the impossibility of dislodging the enemy, began to menace his communications—but the moment Merci perceived this, he broke up his camp and retired beyond the Black mountains.

# MAXIM XVII

In a war of march and manœuvre, if you would avoid a battle with a superior army, it is necessary to entrench every night, and occupy a good defensive position. Those natural positions which are ordinarily met with, are not sufficient to protect an army against superior numbers without recourse to art.

NOTE.

The campaign of the French and Spanish army, commanded by the Duke of Berwick, against the Portuguese, in the year 1706, affords a good lesson on this subject. The two armies made almost the tour of Spain. They began the campaign near Badajoz, and after manœuvring across both Castiles, finished it in the kingdoms of Valencia and Murcia. The Duke of Berwick encamped his army eighty-five times, and although the campaign passed without a general action, he took about ten thousand prisoners from the enemy. Marshal Turenne also made a fine campaign of manœuvre against the Count Montécuculli, in 1675.

The imperial army having made its arrangements to pass the Rhine at Strasburg, Turenne used all diligence, and, throwing a bridge over the river near the village of Ottenheim, three leagues below Strasburg, he crossed with the French army, and encamped close to the little town of Vilstet, which he occupied. This position covered the bridge of Strasburg, so that, by this manœuvre, Turenne deprived the enemy of all approach to that city.

Upon this, Montécuculli made a movement with his whole army, threatening the bridge at Ottenheim, by which the French received their provisions from upper Alsace.

As soon as Turenne discovered the design of the enemy, he left a detachment at Vilstet, and made a rapid march with his whole force upon the village of Altenheim. This intermediate position between the two bridges, which he wished to preserve, gave him the advantage of being able to succor either of these posts before the enemy had time to carry them. Montécuculli seeing that any successful attack upon the bridges was not to be expected, resolved to pass the Rhine below Strasburg, and with this view returned to his first position at Offenburg. Marshal Turenne, who followed all the movements of the Austrian army, brought back his army also to Vilstet.

In the meantime, this attempt of the enemy having convinced the French general of the danger to which his bridge had exposed him, removed it nearer to that of Strasburg, in order to diminish the extent of ground he had to defend.

Montécuculli, having commanded the magistrates of Strasburg to collect materials for a bridge, moved to Scherzheim to receive them; but Turenne again defeated his projects by taking a position at Freistett, where he occupied the islands of the Rhine, and immediately constructed a stockade.

Thus it was that, during the whole of this campaign, Turenne succeeded in gaining the initiative of the enemy, and obliging him to follow his movements. He succeeded, also, by a rapid march, in cutting off Montécuculli from the Town of Offenburg, whence he drew his supplies, and would no doubt have prevented the Austrian general from effecting his junction with the corps of Caprara, had not a cannon-shot terminated this great man's life.

### MAXIM XVIII

A general of ordinary talent occupying a bad position, and surprised by a superior force, seeks his safety in retreat; but a great captain supplies all deficiencies by his courage, and marches boldly to meet the attack. By this means he disconcerts his adversary; and if the latter shows any irresolution in his movements, a skilful leader, profiting by his indecision, may even hope for victory, or at least employ the day in manœuvring—at night he entrenches himself, or falls back to a better position. By this determined conduct he maintains the honor of his arms, the first essential to all military superiority.

NOTE.

In 1653, Marshal Turenne was surprised by the Prince of Condé, in a position where his army was completely compromised. He had the power, indeed, by an immediate retreat, of covering himself by the Somme, which he possessed the means of crossing at Peronne, and whence he was distant only half a league; but, fearing the influence of this retrograde movement on the morale of his army, Turenne balanced all disadvantages by his courage, and marched boldly to meet the enemy with very inferior forces. After marching a league, he found an advantageous position, where he made every disposition for a battle. It was three o'clock in the afternoon; but the Spaniards, exhausted with fatigue, hesitated to attack him, and Turenne having covered himself with entrenchments during the night, the enemy no longer dared to risk a general action, and broke up his camp.

### MAXIM XIX

The transition from the defensive to the offensive is one of the most delicate operations.

NOTE.

By studying the first campaign of Napoleon in Italy, we can learn what genius and boldness may effect in passing with an army from the defensive to the offensive. The army of the allies, commanded by General Beaulieu, was provided with every means that could render it formidable. Its force amounted to eighty thousand men, and two hundred pieces of cannon. The French army, on the contrary, could number scarcely thirty thousand men under arms, and thirty pieces of cannon. For some time there had been no issue of meat, and even the bread was irregularly supplied. The infantry was ill clothed, the cavalry wretchedly mounted. All the draught-horses had perished from want, so that the service of the artillery was performed by mules. To remedy these evils, large disbursements were necessary; and such was the state of the finances, that the government had only been able to furnish two thousand louis in specie for the opening of the campaign. The French army could not possibly exist in this state. To advance or retreat was absolutely necessary. Aware of the advantage of surprising the enemy at the very outset of the campaign by some decisive blow, Napoleon prepared for it by recasting the morale of his army.

In a proclamation full of energy, he reminded them that an ignoble death alone remained for them, if they continued on the defensive; that they had nothing to expect from France, but everything to hope from victory. "Abundance courts you in the fertile plains of Italy," said he; "are you deficient, soldiers, in constancy or in courage?" Profiting by the moment of enthusiasm which he had inspired, Napoleon concentrated his forces in order to fall with his whole weight on the different corps of the enemy. Immediately afterward, the battles of Montenotte, Milesimo, and Mondovi, added fresh confidence to the high opinion already entertained by the soldier for his chief; and that army which only a few days ago was encamped amid barren rocks, and consumed by famine, already aspired to the conquest of Italy. In one month after the opening of the campaign, Napoleon had terminated the war with the King of Sardinia, and conquered the Milanese. Rich cantonments soon dispelled from the recollection of the French soldier the misery and fatigue attendant on this rapid march, while a vigilant administration of the resources of the country reorganized the materiel of the French army, and created the means necessary for the attainment of future success.

## MAXIM XX

It may be laid down as a principle, that the line of operation should not be abandoned; but it is one of the most skilful manœuvres in war, to know how to change it, when circumstances authorize or render this necessary. An army which changes skilfully its line of operation deceives the enemy, who becomes ignorant where to look for its rear, or upon what weak points it is assailable.

NOTE.

Frederick sometimes changed his line of operation in the middle of a campaign; but he was enabled to do this, because he was manœuvring at that time in the centre of Germany—an abundant country, capable of supplying all the wants of his army in case his communications with Prussia were intercepted.

Marshal Turenne, in the campaign of 1746, gave up his line of communication to the allies in the same manner; but, like Frederick, he was carrying on the war at this time in the centre of Germany, and having fallen with his whole forces upon Rain, he took the precaution of securing to himself a depôt upon which to establish his base of operation.

By a series of manœuvres, marked alike by audacity and genius, he subsequently compelled the imperial army to abandon its magazines, and retire into Austria for winter quarters.

But these are examples which it appears to me should only be imitated when we have taken full measure of the capacity of our adversary, and above all, when we see no reason to apprehend an insurrection in the country to which we transfer the theatre of war.

## MAXIM XXI

When an army carries with it a battering train, or large convoys of sick and wounded, it cannot march by too short a line upon its depôts.

NOTE.

It is above all in mountainous countries, and in those interspersed with woods and marshes, that it is of importance to observe this maxim; for, the convoys and means of transport being frequently embarrassed in defiles, an enemy by manœuvring may easily disperse the escorts, or make even a successful attack upon the whole army, when it is obliged, from the nature of the country, to march in an extended column.

## MAXIM XXII

The art of encamping in position is the same as taking up the line in order of battle in this position. To this end, the artillery should be advantageously placed, ground should be selected which is not commanded or liable to be turned, and, as far as possible, the guns should cover and command the surrounding country.

NOTE.

Frederick has remarked that, in order to be assured that your camp is well placed, you should see if, by making a small movement, you can oblige the enemy to make a greater; or, if after having forced him to retrograde one march you can compel him to fall back another.

In defensive war, all camps should be entrenched in the front and wings of the position they occupy, and care should be taken that the rear is left perfectly open. If you are threatened with being turned, arrangements should be made beforehand for taking up a more distant position; and you should profit by any disorder in the enemy's line of march, to make an attempt upon his artillery or baggage.

## MAXIM XXIII

When you are occupying a position which the enemy threatens to surround, collect all your force immediately, and menace him with an offensive movement. By this manœuvre, you will prevent him from detaching and annoying your flanks in case you should judge it necessary to retire.

NOTE.

This was the manœuvre practised by General Desaix, in 1798, near Radstadt. He made up for inferiority in numbers by audacity, and maintained himself the whole day in position in spite of the vigorous attacks of the Archduke Charles. At night he effected his retreat in good order, and took up a position in the rear.

It was in accordance, also, with this principle, in the same campaign, that General Moreau gave battle at Biberach, to secure his retreat by the passes of the Black mountains. A few days after, he fought at Schliengen with the same object. Placed in a good defensive position, he menaced the Archduke Charles by a sudden return to the offensive, while his artillery and baggage were passing the Rhine by the bridge of Huningen, and he was making all the necessary arrangements for retiring behind that river himself.

Here, however, I would observe, that the execution of such offensive demonstrations should be deferred always till toward the evening, in order that you may not be compromised by engaging too early in a combat which you cannot long maintain with success.

Night, and the uncertainty of the enemy after an affair of this kind, will always favor your retreat, if it is judged necessary; but, with a view to mask the operation more effectually, fires should be lighted all along the lines, to deceive the enemy and prevent him from discovering this retrograde movement, for in a retreat it is a great advantage to gain a march upon your adversary.

## MAXIM XXIV

Never lose sight of this maxim: that you should establish your cantonments at the most distant and best-protected point from the enemy, especially where a surprise is possible. By this means you will have time to unite all your forces before he can attack you.

NOTE.

In the campaign of 1745, Marshal Turenne lost the battle of Marienthal, by neglecting this principle; for if, instead of reassembling his divisions at Erbsthausen, he had rallied his troops at Mergentheim, behind the Tauber, his army would have been much sooner reunited; and Count Merci, in place of finding only three thousand men to fight at Erbsthausen (of which he was well informed), would have had the whole French army to attack in a position covered by a river.

Some one having indiscreetly asked Viscount Turenne how he had lost the battle of Marienthal: "By my own fault," replied the marshal; "but," added he, "when a man has committed no faults in war, he can only have been engaged in it but a short time."

## MAXIM XXV

When two armies are in order of battle, and one has to retire over a bridge, while the other has the circumference of the circle open, all the advantages are in favor of the latter. It is then a general should show boldness, strike a decided blow, and manœuvre upon the flank of his enemy. The victory is in his hands.

NOTE.

This was the position of the French army at the famous battle of Leipzig, which terminated the campaign of 1813 so fatally for Napoleon; for the battle of Hanau was of no consequence, comparatively, in the desperate situation of that army.

It strikes me that, in a situation like that of the French army previous to the battle of Leipzig, a general should never calculate upon any of those lucky chances which may arise out of a return to the offensive, but that he should rather adopt every possible means to secure his retreat. With this view, he should immediately cover himself with good entrenchments, to enable him to repel with inferior numbers the attack of the enemy, while his own equipments are crossing the river. As fast as the troops reach the other side, they should occupy positions to protect the passage of the rear guard, and this last should be covered by a tête de pont as soon as the army breaks up its camp. During the wars of the Revolution, too little regard was paid to entrenchments; and it is for this reason we have seen large armies dispersed after a single reverse, and the fate of nations compromised by the issue of one battle.

## MAXIM XXVI

It is contrary to all true principle, to make corps, which have no communication with each other, act separately against a central force whose communications are cut off.

NOTE.

The Austrians lost the battle of Hohenlinden by neglecting this principle. The imperial army, under the orders of the archduke John, was divided into four columns, which had to march through an immense forest, previous to their junction in the plain of Anzing, where they intended to surprise the French. But these different corps, having no direct communication, found themselves compelled to engage separately with an enemy who had taken the precaution of concentrating his masses, and who could move them with facility in a country with which he had been long previously acquainted.

Thus the Austrian army, enclosed in the defiles of the forest with its whole train of artillery and baggage, was attacked in its flanks and rear, and the archduke John was only enabled to rally his dispersed and shattered divisions under cover of the night.

The trophies obtained by the French army on this day were immense. They consisted of eleven thousand prisoners, one hundred pieces of cannon, several stand of colors, and all the baggage of the enemy.

The battle of Hohenlinden decided the fate of the campaign of 1800, and Moreau's brilliant and well-merited success placed him in the rank of the first general of the age.

## MAXIM XXVII

When an army is driven from a first position, the retreating columns should rally always sufficiently in the rear, to prevent any interruption from the enemy. The greatest disaster that can happen, is when the columns are attacked in detail, and before their junction.

NOTE.

One great advantage which results from rallying your columns on a point far removed from the field of battle, or from the position previously occupied, is, that the enemy is uncertain as to the direction you mean to take.

If he divides his force to pursue you, he exposes himself to see his detachments beaten in detail, especially if you have exerted all due diligence, and have effected the junction of your troops in sufficient time to get between his columns and disperse them one after the other.

It was by a manœuvre of this kind in the campaign of Italy, in 1799, that General Melas gained the battle of Genola.

General Championet commanded the French army, and endeavored to cut off the communication of the Austrians with Turin, by employing corps which manœuvred separately to get into their rear. Melas, who divined his project, made a retrograde march, by which he persuaded his adversary he was in full retreat, although the real object of his movement was to concentrate his forces at the point fixed for the junction of the different detachments of the French army, and which he beat and dispersed, one after another, by his great superiority in numbers. The result of this manœuvre, in which the Austrian general displayed vigor, decision, and foresight, secured to him the peaceable possession of Piedmont.

It was also by the neglect of this principle that General Beaulieu, who commanded the Austro-Sardinian army in the campaign of 1796, lost the battle of Milesimo after that of Montenotte.

His object, in endeavoring to rally his different corps upon Milesimo, was, to cover the high roads of Turin and Milan; but Napoleon, aware of the advantages arising from the ardor of troops emboldened by recent success, attacked him before he could assemble his divisions, and, by a series of skilful manœuvres, succeeded in separating the combined armies. They retired in the greatest disorder—the one by the road of Milan, the other by that of Turin.

## MAXIM XXVIII

No force should be detached on the eve of a battle, because affairs may change during the night, either by the retreat of the enemy, or by the arrival of large reinforcements to enable him to resume the offensive, and counteract your previous arrangements.

NOTE.

In 1796, the army of the Sambre and Meuse, commanded by General Jourdan, effected a retreat, which was rendered still more difficult by the loss of his line of communication. Seeing, however, that the forces of the archduke Charles were scattered, Jourdan, in order to accomplish his retreat upon Frankfort, resolved to open himself a way by Wurtzburg, where there were at that moment only two divisions of the Austrian army. This movement would have been attended with success, if the French general, believing he had simply these two divisions to contend with, had not committed the error of separating himself from the corps of Lefevre—which he left at Schweinfurt to cover the only direct communication of the army with its base of operation.

The commission of this fault at the outset, added to some slowness in the march of the French general, secured the victory to the archduke, who hastened to concentrate his forces.

The arrival of the two divisions, also, of Kray and Wartesleben, during the battle, enabled him to oppose fifty thousand men to the French army, which scarcely numbered thirty thousand combatants. This last was consequently beaten, and obliged to continue its retreat by the mountains of Fuldes, where the badness of the roads could be equalled only by the difficulty of the country.

The division of Lefevre, amounting to fourteen thousand men, would, in all probability, have turned the scale in favor of Jourdan, had the latter not unfortunately conceived that two divisions only were opposing his passage to Wurtzburg.

## MAXIM XXIX

When you have resolved to fight a battle, collect your whole force. Dispense with nothing. A single battalion sometimes decides the day.

NOTE.

I think it here desirable to observe, that it is prudent before a battle to fix upon some point in rear of the reserve for the junction of the different detachments; for if, from unforeseen circumstances, these detachments should be prevented from joining before the action has commenced, they might be exposed, in case a retrograde movement should be found necessary, to the masses of the enemy. It is desirable also to keep the enemy in ignorance of these reinforcements, in order to employ them with greater effect. "A seasonable reinforcement," says Frederick, "renders the success of a battle certain, because the enemy will always imagine it stronger than it really is, and lose courage accordingly."

## MAXIM XXX

Nothing is so rash or so contrary to principle, as to make a flank march before an army in position, especially when this army occupies heights at the foot of which you are forced to defile.

NOTE.

It was by a neglect of this principle that Frederick was beaten at Kollin in the first campaign of 1757. Notwithstanding prodigies of valor, the Prussians lost fifteen thousand men and a great portion of their artillery, while the loss of the Austrians did not exceed five thousand men. The consequence of this battle was more unfortunate still, since it obliged the King of Prussia to raise the siege of Prague, and to evacuate Bohemia.

It was also by making a flank march before the Prussian army, that the French lost the disgraceful battle of Rosbach.

This imprudent movement was still more to be reprehended, because the Prince de Soubise, who commanded the French army, was so negligent as to manœuvre, without either advanced guards or flanking corps, in presence of the enemy. The result was, that his army, consisting of fifty thousand men, was beaten by six battalions and thirty squadrons. The French lost seven thousand men, twenty-seven standards, and a great number of cannon. The Prussians had only three hundred men disabled.

Thus, by having forgotten this principle, that a flank march is never to be made before an enemy in line of battle, Frederick lost his army at Kollin; and Soubise, at Rosbach, lost both his army and his honor.

## MAXIM XXXI

When you determine to risk a battle, reserve to yourself every possible chance of success, more particularly if you have to deal with an adversary of superior talent; for if you are beaten, even in the midst of your magazines and your communications, wo to the vanquished!

NOTE.

"We should make war," says Marshal Saxe, "without leaving anything to hazard, and in this especially consists the talent of a general. But when we have incurred the risk of a battle, we should know how to profit by the victory, and not merely content ourselves, according to custom, with possession of the field."

It was by neglecting to follow up the first success, that the Austrian army, after gaining the field of Marengo, saw itself compelled on the following day to evacuate the whole of Italy.

General Melas, observing the French in retreat, left the direction of the movements of his army to the chief of his staff, and retired to Alexandria to repose from the fatigues of the day. Colonel Zach, equally convinced with his general that the French army was completely broken, and consisted only of fugitives, formed the divisions in column of route.

By this arrangement, the imperial army prepared to enter upon its victorious march in a formation not less than three miles in depth.

It was near four o'clock when General Desaix rejoined the French army with his division. His presence restored in some degree an equality between the contending forces; and yet Napoleon hesitated for a moment whether to resume the offensive, or to make use of this corps to secure his retreat. The ardor of the troops to return to the charge, decided his irresolution. He rode rapidly along the front of his divisions, and addressing the soldiers—"We have retired far enough for to-day," said he; "you know I always sleep upon the field of battle!"

The army, with unanimous shout, proclaimed to him a promise of victory. Napoleon resumed the offensive. The Austrian advance guard, panic-struck at the sight of a formidable and unbroken body presenting itself suddenly at a point where, a few moments before, only fugitives were to be seen, went to the right about, and carried disorder into the mass of its columns. Attacked immediately afterward, with impetuosity, in its front and flanks, the Austrian army was completely routed.

Marshal Daun experienced nearly the same fate as General Melas, at the battle of Torgau, in the campaign of 1760.

The position of the Austrian army was excellent. It had its left upon Torgau, its right on the plateau of Siptitz, and its front covered by a large sheet of water.

Frederick proposed to turn its right in order to make an attack upon the rear. For this purpose he divided his army into two corps, the one under the orders of Ziethen, with instructions to attack in front, following the edge of the water; the other under his own immediate command, with which he set out to turn the right of the Austrians. But Marshal Daun having had intimation of the movements of the enemy, changed his front by countermarching, and was thus enabled to repel the attacks of Frederick, whom he obliged to retreat. The two corps of the Prussian army had been acting without communication. Ziethen, in the meantime, hearing the fire recede, concluded that the king had been beaten, and commenced a movement by his left in order to rejoin him; but falling in with two battalions of the reserve, the Prussian general profited by this reinforcement to resume the offensive. Accordingly he renewed the attack with vigor, got possession of the plateau of Siptitz, and soon after of the whole field of battle. The sun had already set when the King of Prussia received the news of this unexpected good fortune. He returned in all haste, took advantage of the night to restore order in his disorganized army, and the day after the battle occupied Torgau.

Marshal Daun was receiving congratulations upon his victory, when he heard that the Prussians had resumed the offensive. He immediately commanded a retreat, and at daybreak the Austrians repassed the Elbe with the loss of twelve thousand men, eight thousand prisoners, and forty-five pieces of cannon.

After the battle of Marengo, General Melas, although in the midst of his fortresses and magazines, saw himself compelled to abandon everything, in order to save the wreck of his army.

General Mack capitulated after the battle of Ulm, although in the centre of his own country.

The Prussians, in spite of their depôts and reserves, were obliged, after the battle of Jena, and the French after that of Waterloo, to lay down their arms.

Hence, we may conclude that the misfortune that results from the loss of a battle, does not consist so much in the destruction of men and of materiel as in the discouragement which follows this disaster. The courage and confidence of the victors augment in proportion as those of the vanquished diminish; and whatever may be the resources of an army, it will be found that a retreat will degenerate rapidly into a rout unless the general-in-chief shall succeed, by combining boldness with skill, and perseverance with firmness, in restoring the morale of his army.

## MAXIM XXXII

The duty of an advanced guard does not consist in advancing or retiring, but in manœuvring. An advanced guard should be composed of light cavalry, supported by a reserve of heavy cavalry, and by battalions of infantry, supported also by artillery. An advanced guard should consist of picked troops, and the general officers, officers and men, should be selected for their respective capabilities and knowledge. A corps deficient in instruction is only an embarrassment to an advanced guard.

NOTE.

It was the opinion of Frederick that an advanced guard should be composed of detachments of troops of all arms. The commander should possess skill in the choice of ground, and he should take care to be instantly informed, by means of numerous patrols, of everything passing in the enemy's camp.

In war, it is not the business of an advanced guard to fight, but to observe the enemy, in order to cover the movements of the army. When in pursuit, the advanced guard should charge with vigor, and cut off the baggage and insulated corps of the retiring enemy. For this purpose, it should be reinforced with all the disposable light cavalry of the army.

## MAXIM XXXIII

It is contrary to the usages of war to allow parks or batteries of artillery to enter a defile, unless you hold the other extremity. In case of retreat, the guns will embarrass your movements and be lost. They should be left in position, under a sufficient escort, until you are master of the opening.

NOTE.

Nothing encumbers the march of an army so much as a quantity of baggage. In the campaign of 1796, Napoleon abandoned his battering train under the walls of Mantua, after spiking the guns and destroying the carriages. By this sacrifice, he acquired a facility of manœuvring rapidly his little army, and obtained the initiative as well as a general superiority over the numerous but divided forces of Marshal Wurmser.

In 1799, during his retreat in Italy, General Moreau being compelled to manœuvre among the mountains, preferred separating himself entirely from his reserve artillery, which he directed upon France by the Col de Fenestrelle, rather than embarrass his march with this part of his equipment.

These are the examples we should follow; for if, by a rapidity of march, and a facility of concentration upon decisive points, the victory is gained, the materiel of an army is soon re-established. But if, on the other hand, we are beaten and compelled to retreat, it will be difficult to save our equipments, and we may have reason to congratulate ourselves that we abandoned them in time to prevent them from augmenting the trophies of the enemy.

## MAXIM XXXIV

It should be laid down as a principle, never to leave intervals by which the enemy can penetrate between corps formed in order of battle, unless it be to draw him into a snare.

NOTE.

In the campaign of 1757, the Prince of Lorraine, who was covering Prague with the Austrian army, perceived the Prussians threatening, by a flank movement, to turn his right. He immediately ordered a partial change of front by throwing back the infantry of that wing, so as to form a right angle with the rest of the line. But this manœuvre being executed in presence of the enemy, was not effected without some disorder. The heads of the columns having marched too quick, caused the rear to lengthen out, and when the line was formed to the right, a large interval appeared at the salient angle. Frederick, observing this error, hastened to take advantage of it. He directed his centre corps, commanded by the Duke of Bevern, to throw itself into this opening, and by this manœuvre decided the fate of the battle.

The Prince of Lorraine returned to Prague, beaten and pursued, with the loss of sixteen thousand men and two hundred pieces of cannon.

It should be observed at the same time, that this operation of throwing a corps into the intervals made by an army in time of battle, should never be attempted unless you are at least equal in force, and have an opportunity of outflanking the enemy on the one side or the other; for it is then only you can hope to divide his army in the centre, and insulate the wings entirely. If you are inferior in number, you run the risk of being stopped by the reverses, and overpowered by the enemy's wings, which may deploy upon your flanks and surround you.

It was by this manœuvre that the Duke of Berwick gained the battle of Almanza, in the year 1707, in Spain.

The Anglo-Portuguese army, under the command of Lord Galloway, came to invest Villena. Marshal Berwick, who commanded the French and Spanish army, quitted his camp at Montalegre, and moved upon this town to raise the siege. At his approach, the English general, eager to fight a battle, advanced to meet him in the plains of Almanza. The issue was long doubtful. The first line, commanded by the Duke of Popoli, having been broken, the Chevalier d'Asfeldt, who had charge of the second, drew up his masses with large intervals between them; and when the English, who were in pursuit of the first line, reached these reserves, he took advantage of their disorder to attack them in flank and defeated them entirely.

Marshal Berwick, perceiving the success of this manœuvre, threw open his front, and deploying upon the enemy's flanks, while the reserve sustained the attack in front, and the cavalry manœuvred in their rear, obtained a complete victory.

Lord Galloway, wounded and pursued, collected with difficulty the remains of his army, and took shelter with them in Tortosa.

## MAXIM XXXV

Encampments of the same army should always be formed so as to protect each other.

NOTE.

At the battle of Dresden, in the campaign of 1813, the camp of the allies, although advantageously placed upon the heights on the left bank of the Elbe, was nevertheless extremely defective, from being traversed longitudinally by a deep ravine, which separated the left wing completely from the centre and the right. This vicious arrangement did not escape the penetrating eye of Napoleon. He instantly directed the whole of his cavalry and two corps of infantry against the insulated wing, attacked it with superior numbers, overthrew it, and took ten thousand prisoners, before it was possible to come to its support.

## MAXIM XXXVI

When the enemy's army is covered by a river, upon which he holds several têtes de pont, do not attack in front. This would divide your force and expose you to be turned. Approach the river in echelon of columns, in such a manner that the leading column shall be the only one the enemy can attack, without offering you his flank. In the meantime, let your light troops occupy the bank, and when you have decided on the point of passage, rush upon it and fling across your bridge. Observe that the point of passage should be always at a distance from the leading echelon, in order to deceive the enemy.

NOTE.

If you occupy a town or a village on the bank of a river, opposite to that held by the enemy, it is an advantage to make this spot the crossing point, because it is easier to cover your carriages and reserve artillery, as well as to mask the construction of your bridge, in a town, than in the open country. It is also a great advantage to pass a river opposite a village, when the latter is only weakly occupied by the enemy; because as soon as the advanced guard reaches the other side, it carries this post, makes a lodgment, and by throwing up a few defensive works, converts it easily into a tête de pont. By this means, the rest of the army is enabled to effect the passage with facility.

## MAXIM XXXVII

From the moment you are master of a position which commands the opposite bank, facilities are acquired for effecting the passage of the river; above all, if this position is sufficiently extensive to place upon it artillery in force. This advantage is diminished, if the river is more than three hundred toises (or six hundred yards) in breadth, because the distance being out of the range of grape, it is easy for the troops which defend the passage to line the bank and get under cover. Hence it follows that if the grenadiers, ordered to pass the river for the protection of the bridge, should reach the other side, they would be destroyed by the fire of the enemy; because his batteries, placed at the distance of two hundred toises from the landing, are capable of a most destructive effect, although removed above five hundred toises from the batteries of the crossing force. Thus the advantage of the artillery would be exclusively his. For the same reason, the passage is impracticable, unless you succeed in surprising the enemy, and are protected by an intermediate island, or, unless you are able to take advantage of an angle in the river, to establish a crossfire upon his works. In this case, the island or angle forms a natural tête de pont, and gives the advantage in artillery to the attacking army.

When a river is less than sixty toises (or one hundred and twenty yards) in breadth, and you have a post upon the other side, the troops which are thrown across derive such advantages from the protection of your artillery, that, however small the angle may be, it is impossible for the enemy to prevent the establishment of a bridge. In this case, the most skilful generals, when they have discovered the project of their adversary, and brought their own army to the point of crossing, usually content themselves with opposing the passage of the bridge, by forming a semicircle round its extremity, as round the opening of a defile, and removing to the distance of three or four hundred toises from the fire of the opposite side.

NOTE.

Frederick observes, that "the passage of great rivers in the presence of the enemy is one of the most delicate operations in war." Success on these occasions depends on secrecy, on the rapidity of the manœuvres, and the punctual execution of the orders given for the movements of each division. To pass such an obstacle in presence of an enemy, and without his knowledge, it is necessary not only that the previous dispositions should be well conceived, but that they should be executed without confusion.

In the campaign of 1705, Prince Eugene, of Savoy, wishing to come to the assistance of the Prince of Piedmont, sought for a favorable point at which to force the passage of the Adda, defended at that time by the French army, under the command of the Duke de Vendome.

After having selected an advantageous situation, Prince Eugene erected a battery of twenty pieces of cannon on a position which commanded the entire of the opposite bank, and covered his infantry by a line of entrenched parallels constructed on the slope of the declivity.

They were working vigorously at the bridge, when the Duke de Vendome appeared with his whole army. At first he seemed determined to oppose its construction, but after having examined the position of Prince Eugene, he judged this to be impracticable.

He therefore placed his army out of reach of the prince's batteries, resting both his wings upon the river, so as to form a bow, of which the Adda was the cord. He then covered himself with entrenchments and abattis, and was thus enabled to charge the enemy's columns whenever they debouched from the bridge, and to beat them in detail.

Eugene, having reconnoitred the position of the French, considered the passage impossible. He therefore withdrew the bridge, and broke up his camp during the night.

It was by this manœuvre, also, that, in the campaign of 1809, the Archduke Charles compelled the French to reoccupy the isle of Lobau, after having debouched on the left bank of the Danube. The march of the Archduke Charles was wholly concentric. He menaced Grosaspern with his right, Esling with his centre, and Enzersdorf with his left.

His army, with both wings resting on the Danube, formed a semicircle around Esling. Napoleon immediately attacked and broke the centre of the Austrians; but after having forced their first line, he found himself arrested by the reserves. In the meantime, the bridges upon the Danube had been destroyed, and several of his corps, with their parks of artillery, were still on the right bank. This disappointment, joined to the favorable position of the Austrians, decided Napoleon to re-enter the isle of Lobau, where he had previously constructed a line of field-works, so as to give it all the advantages of a well entrenched camp.

## MAXIM XXXVIII

It is difficult to prevent an enemy, supplied with pontoons, from crossing a river. When the object of an army, which defends the passage, is to cover a siege, the moment the general has ascertained his inability to oppose the passage, he should take measures to arrive before the enemy, at an intermediate position between the river he defends and the place he desires to cover.

NOTE.

Here we may observe, that this intermediate position should be reconnoitred, or rather, well entrenched beforehand; for the enemy will be unable to make an offensive movement against the corps employed in the siege, until he has beaten the army of observation; and the latter, under cover of its camp, may always await a favorable opportunity to attack him in flank or in rear.

Besides, the army which is once entrenched in this manner, has the advantage of being concentrated; while that of the enemy must act in detachments, if he wishes to cover his bridge, and watch the movements of the army of observation, so as to enable him to attack the besieging corps in its lines, without being exposed to an attempt on his rear, or being menaced with the loss of his bridge.


## MAXIM XXXIX

In the campaign of 1645, Turenne was attacked with his army before Philipsburg by a very superior force. There was no bridge here over the Rhine, but he took advantage of the ground between the river and the place to establish his camp. This should serve as a lesson to engineer officers, not merely in the construction of fortresses, but of têtes de pont. A space should always be left between the fortress and the river, where an army may form and rally without being obliged to throw itself into the place, and thereby compromise its security. An army retiring upon Mayence before a pursuing enemy, is necessarily compromised; for this reason, because it requires more than a day to pass the bridge, and because the lines of Cassel are too confined to admit an army to remain there without being blocked up. Two hundred toises should have been left between that place and the Rhine. It is essential that all têtes de pont before great rivers should be constructed upon this principle, otherwise they will prove a very inefficient assistance to protect the passage of a retreating army. Têtes de pont, as laid down in our schools, are of use only for small rivers, the passage of which is comparatively short.

NOTE.

Marshal Saxe, in the campaign of 1741, having passed the Moldau in quest of a detached corps of fourteen thousand men, which was about to throw itself into Prague, left a thousand infantry upon that river, with orders to entrench themselves upon a height directly opposite the tête de pont. By this precaution, the marshal secured his retreat, and also the facility of repassing the bridge without disorder, by rallying his divisions between the entrenched height and the tête de pont.

Were these examples unknown to the generals of modern times, or are they disposed to think such precautions superfluous?


## MAXIM XL

Fortresses are equally useful in offensive and defensive warfare. It is true, they will not in themselves arrest an army, but they are an excellent means of retarding, embarrassing, weakening and annoying a victorious enemy.

NOTE.

The brilliant success of the allied armies in the campaign of 1814, has given to many military men a false idea of the real value of fortresses.

The formidable bodies which crossed the Rhine and the Alps at this period, were enabled to spare large detachments to blockade the strong places that covered the frontiers of France, without materially affecting the numerical superiority of the army which marched upon the capital. This army was in a condition, therefore, to act, without the fear of being menaced in its line of retreat.

But at no period of military history were the armies of Europe so combined before, or governed so entirely by one common mind in the attainment of a single object. Under these circumstances, the line of fortresses which surround France was rendered unavailable during the campaign; but it would be very imprudent, therefore, to conclude that a frontier guarded by numerous fortresses may be passed with impunity; or that battles may be fought with these places in your rear, without previously besieging, or at least investing them with sufficient forces.

## MAXIM XLI

There are only two ways of insuring the success of a siege. The first, to begin by beating the enemy's army employed to cover the place, forcing it out of the field, and throwing its remains beyond some great natural obstacle, such as a chain of mountains, or large river. Having accomplished this object, an army of observation should be placed behind the natural obstacle, until the trenches are finished and the place taken.

But if it be desired to take the place in presence of a relieving army, without risking a battle, then the whole materiel and equipment for a siege are necessary to begin with, together with ammunition and provisions for the presumed period of its duration, and also lines of contravallation and circumvallation, aided by all the localities of heights, woods, marshes and inundations.

Having no longer occasion to keep up communications with your depôts, it is now only requisite to hold in check the relieving army. For this purpose, an army of observation should be formed, whose business it is never to lose sight of that of the enemy, and which, while it effectually bars all access to the place, has always time enough to arrive upon his flanks or rear in case he should attempt to steal a march.

It is to be remembered, too, that by profiting judiciously by the lines of contravallation, a portion of the besieging army will always be available in giving battle to the approaching enemy.

Upon the same general principle, when a place is to be besieged in presence of an enemy's army, it is necessary to cover the siege by lines of circumvallation.

If the besieging force is of numerical strength enough (after leaving a corps before the place four times the amount of the garrison) to cope with the relieving army, it may remove more than one day's march from the place; but if it be inferior in numbers after providing for the siege, as above stated, it should remain only a short day's march from the spot, in order to fall back upon its lines, if necessary, or receive succor in case of attack.

If the investing corps and army of observation are only equal when united to the relieving force, the besieging army should remain entire within, or near its lines, and push the works and the siege with the greatest activity.

NOTE.

"When we undertake a siege," says Montécuculli, "we should not seek to place ourselves opposite the weakest part of the fortress, but at the point most favorable for establishing a camp and executing the designs we have in view."

This maxim was well understood by the Duke of Berwick. Sent to form the siege of Nice in 1706, he determined to attack on the side of Montalban, contrary to the advice of Vauban, and even to the orders of the king. Having a very small army at his disposal, he began by securing his camp. This he did by constructing redoubts upon the heights that shut in the space between the Var and the Paillon, two rivers which supported his flanks. By this means, he protected himself against a surprise; for the Duke of Savoy, having the power of debouching suddenly by the Col de Tende, it was necessary that the marshal should be enabled to assemble his forces, so as to move rapidly upon his adversary, and fight him before he got into position; otherwise his inferiority in numbers would have obliged him to raise the siege.

When Marshal Saxe was besieging Brussels, with only twenty-eight thousand men, opposed to a garrison of twelve thousand, he received intelligence that the Prince of Waldeck was assembling his forces to raise the siege. Not being strong enough to form an army of observation, the marshal reconnoitred a field of battle on the little river Voluve, and made all the necessary dispositions for moving rapidly to the spot, in case of the approach of the enemy. By this means he was prepared to receive his adversary without discontinuing the operations of the siege.

## MAXIM XLII

Feuquière says that "we should never wait for the enemy in the lines of circumvallation, but we should go out and attack him." He is in error. There is no authority in war without exception; and it would be dangerous to proscribe the principle of awaiting the enemy within the lines of circumvallation.

NOTE.

During the siege of Mons, in 1691, the Prince of Orange assembled his army, and advanced as far as Notre Dame de Halle, making a demonstration to succor the place. Louis XIV, who commanded the siege in person, called a council of war to deliberate on what was to be done in case the Prince of Orange approached. The opinion of Marshal Luxembourg was to remain within the lines of circumvallation, and that opinion prevailed.

The marshal laid it down as a principle that, when the besieging army is not strong enough to defend the whole extent of circumvallation, it should quit the lines and advance to meet the enemy; but when it is strong enough to encamp in two lines around a place, that it is better to profit by a good entrenchment—more especially as by this means the siege is not interrupted.

In 1658, Marshal Turenne was besieging Dunkirk. He had already opened the trenches, when the Spanish army, under the orders of the Prince Don Juan, Condé, and D'Hocquincourt, appeared in sight, and took post upon the Downs, at a distance of a league from his lines. Turenne had the superiority in numbers, and he determined to quit his entrenchments. He had other advantages also. The enemy was without artillery, and their superiority in cavalry was rendered useless by the unfavorable nature of the ground. It was, therefore, of great importance to beat the Spanish army before it had time to entrench itself and bring up its artillery. The victory gained by the French on this occasion justified all the combinations of Marshal Turenne.

When Marshal Berwick was laying siege to Philipsburg, in 1733, he had reason to apprehend that the Prince of Savoy would attack him with all the forces of the empire before its termination. The marshal, therefore, after having made his disposition of the troops intended for the siege, formed, with the rest of his army, a corps of observation to make head against Prince Eugene, in case the latter should choose to attack him in his lines, or attempt a diversion on the Moselle or Upper Rhine. Prince Eugene, having arrived in front of the besieging army, some general officers were of opinion that it was better not to await the enemy in the lines, but to move forward and attack him. But Marshal Berwick, who agreed with the Duke of Luxembourg, that an army which can occupy, completely, good entrenchments is not liable to be forced, persisted in remaining within his works. The result proved that this was also the opinion of Prince Eugene, for he did not dare to attack the entrenchments, which he would not have failed to do if he had any hopes of success.

## MAXIM XLIII

Those who proscribe lines of circumvallation, and all the assistance which the science of the engineer can afford, deprive themselves gratuitously of an auxiliary which is never injurious, almost always useful, and often indispensable. It must be admitted, at the same time, that the principles of field-fortification require improvement. This important branch of the art of war has made no progress since the time of the ancients. It is even inferior at this day to what it was two thousand years ago. Engineer officers should be encouraged in bringing this branch of their art to perfection, and in placing it upon a level with the rest.

NOTE.

"If we are inferior in numbers," says Marshal Saxe, "entrenchments are of no use, for the enemy will bring all his forces to bear upon particular points. If we are of equal strength they are unnecessary also. If we are superior, we do not want them. Then why give ourselves the trouble to entrench?" Notwithstanding this opinion of the inutility of entrenchments, Marshal Saxe often had recourse to them.

In 1797, Generals Provéra and Hohenzollern having presented themselves before Mantua (where Marshal Wurmser was shut up), for the purpose of raising the siege, they were stopped by the lines of contravallation of St. George. This slight obstacle sufficed to afford Napoleon time to arrive from Rivoli and defeat their enterprise. It was in consequence of neglecting to entrench themselves that the French had been obliged to raise the siege in the preceding campaign.

## MAXIM XLIV

If circumstances prevent a sufficient garrison being left to defend a fortified town, which contains an hospital and magazines, at least every means should be employed to secure the citadel against a coup de main.

NOTE.

A few battalions dispersed about a town, inspire no terror; but shut up in the more narrow outline of a citadel, they assume an imposing attitude. For this reason it appears to me that such a precaution is always necessary, not only in fortresses, but wherever there are hospitals or depôts of any kind. Where there is no citadel, some quarter of the town should be fixed upon most favorable for defence, and entrenched in such a manner as to oppose the greatest resistance possible.

## MAXIM XLV

A fortified place can only protect the garrison and detain the enemy for a certain time. When this time has elapsed, and the defences of the place are destroyed, the garrison should lay down its arms. All civilized nations are agreed on this point, and there never has been an argument except with reference to the greater or less degree of defence which a governor is bound to make before he capitulates. At the same time, there are generals—Villars among the number—who are of opinion that a governor should never surrender, but that in the last extremity he should blow up the fortifications, and take advantage of the night to cut his way through the besieging army. Where he is unable to blow up the fortifications, he may always retire, they say, with his garrison, and save the men.

Officers who have adopted this line of conduct, have often brought off three-fourths of their garrison.

NOTE.

In 1705, the French, who were besieged in Haguenau by Count Thungen, found themselves incapable of sustaining an assault. Péri, the governor, who had already distinguished himself by a vigorous defence, despairing of being allowed to capitulate on any terms short of becoming prisoner of war, resolved to abandon the place and cut his way through the besiegers.

In order to conceal his intention more effectually, and while he deceived the enemy, to sound at the same time the disposition of his officers, he assembled a council of war and declared his resolution to die in the breach. Then, under pretext of the extremity to which he was reduced, he commanded the whole garrison under arms; and leaving only a few sharpshooters in the breach, gave the order to march, and set out in silence, under cover of the night, from Haguenau. This audacious enterprise was crowned with success, and Péri reached Saverne without having suffered the smallest loss.

Two fine instances of defence in later times are those of Massena at Genoa, and of Palafox at Saragossa.

The first marched out with arms and baggage, and all the honors of war, after rejecting every summons, and defending himself until hunger alone compelled him to capitulate. The second only yielded after having buried his garrison amid the ruins of the city, which he defended from house to house, until famine and death left him no alternative but to surrender. This siege, which was equally honorable to the French as to the Spaniards, is one of the most memorable in the history of war. In the course of it, Palafox displayed every possible resource which courage and obstinacy can supply in the defence of a fortress.

All real strength is founded in the mind; and on this account I am of opinion that we should be directed in the choice of a governor, less by his genius than his personal character. His most essential qualities should be courage, perseverance, and soldierlike devotedness. Above all, he should possess the talent not only of infusing courage into the garrison, but of kindling a spirit of resistance in the whole population. Where the latter is wanting, however art may multiply the defences of a place, the garrison will be compelled to capitulate after having sustained the first, or at most, the second assault.

## MAXIM XLVI

The keys of a fortress are well worth the retirement of the garrison, when it is resolved to yield only on those conditions. On this principle it is always wiser to grant an honorable capitulation to a garrison which has made a vigorous resistance, than to risk an assault.

NOTE.

Marshal Villars has justly observed, that "no governor of a place should be permitted to excuse himself for surrendering, on the ground of wishing to preserve the king's troops. Every garrison that displays courage will escape being prisoners of war. For there is no general who, however well assured of carrying a place by assault, will not prefer granting terms of capitulation rather than risk the loss of a thousand men in forcing determined troops to surrender."

## MAXIM XLVII

Infantry, cavalry, and artillery, are nothing without each other; therefore, they should always be so disposed in cantonments as to assist each other in case of surprise.

NOTE.

"A general," says Frederick, "should direct his whole attention to the tranquility of his cantonments, in order that the soldier may be relieved from all anxiety, and repose in security from his fatigues. With this view, care should be taken that the troops are able to form rapidly upon ground which has been previously reconnoitered; that the generals remain always with their divisions or brigades, and that the service is carried on throughout with exactness."

Marshal Saxe is of opinion that an army should not be in a hurry to quit its cantonments, but that it should wait till the enemy has exhausted himself with marching, and be ready to fall upon him with fresh troops when he is overcome with fatigue.

I believe, however, that it would be dangerous to trust implicitly to this high authority, for there are many occasions where all the advantage lies in the initiative, more especially when the enemy has been compelled to extend his cantonments, from scarcity of subsistence, and can be attacked before he has time to concentrate his forces.

## MAXIM XLVIII

The formation of infantry in line should be always in two ranks, because the length of the musket only admits of an effective fire in this formation. The discharge of the third rank is not only uncertain, but frequently dangerous to the ranks in its front. In drawing up infantry in two ranks, there should be a supernumerary behind every fourth or fifth file. A reserve should likewise be placed twenty-five paces in rear of each flank.

NOTE.

I am of opinion, if circumstances require a line of infantry to resort to a square, that two-deep is too light a formation to resist the shock of cavalry. However useless the third rank may appear for the purpose of file-firing, it is, notwithstanding necessary, in order to replace the men who fall in the ranks in front; otherwise you would be obliged to close in the files, and by this means leave intervals between the companies, which the cavalry would not fail to penetrate. It appears to me, also, that when infantry is formed in two ranks, the columns will be found to open out in marching to a flank. If it should be considered advantageous behind entrenchments to keep the infantry in two ranks, the third rank should be placed in reserve, and brought forward to relieve the front rank when fatigued, or when the fire is observed to slacken. I am induced to make these remarks, because I have seen an excellent pamphlet which proposes the two-deep formation for infantry as the best. The author supports his opinion by a variety of plausible reasons, but not sufficient, as it appears to me, to answer all the objections that may be offered to this practice.

## MAXIM XLIX

The practice of mixing small bodies of infantry and cavalry together is a bad one, and attended with many inconveniences. The cavalry loses its power of action. It becomes fettered in all its movements. Its energy is destroyed; even the infantry itself is compromised, for on the first movement of the cavalry it is left without support. The best mode of protecting cavalry is to cover its flank.

NOTE.

This also was the opinion of Marshal Saxe. "The weakness of the above formation," says he, "is sufficient in itself to intimidate the platoons of infantry, because they must be lost if the cavalry is beaten."

The cavalry, also, which depends on the infantry for succor, is disconcerted the moment a brisk forward movement carries them out of sight of their supports. Marshal Turenne, and the generals of his time, sometimes employed this order of formation; but that does not, in my opinion, justify a modern author for recommending it in an essay, entitled "Considerations sur l'Art de la Guerre." In fact, this formation has long been abandoned; and, since the introduction of light artillery, it appears to me almost ridiculous to propose it.

## MAXIM L

Charges of cavalry are equally useful at the beginning, the middle, and the end of a battle. They should be made always, if possible, on the flanks of the infantry, especially when the latter is engaged in front.

NOTE.

The Archduke Charles, in speaking of cavalry, recommends that it should be brought in mass upon a decisive point, when the moment for employing it arrives; that is to say, when it can attack with a certainty of success. As the rapidity of its movement enables cavalry to act along the whole line in the same day, the general who commands it should keep it together as much as possible, and avoid dividing it into many detachments. When the nature of the ground admits of cavalry being employed on all points of the line, it is desirable to form it in column behind the infantry, and in a position whence it may be easily directed wherever it is required. If cavalry is intended to cover a position, it should be placed sufficiently in the rear to meet at full speed any advance of troops coming to attack that position. If it is destined to cover the flank of the infantry, it should, for the same reason, be placed directly behind it. As the object of cavalry is purely offensive, it should be a rule to form it at such a distance only from the point of collision as to enable it to acquire its utmost impulse, and arrive at the top of its speed into action. With respect to the cavalry reserve, this should only be employed at the end of a battle, either to render the success more decisive, or to cover the retreat. Napoleon remarks that, at the battle of Waterloo, the cavalry of the guard which composed the reserve, was engaged against his orders. He complains of having been deprived from five o'clock of the use of this reserve, which, when well employed, had so often insured him the victory.

## MAXIM LI

It is the business of cavalry to follow up the victory, and to prevent the beaten enemy from rallying.

NOTE.

Victor or vanquished, it is of the greatest importance to have a body of cavalry in reserve, either to take advantage of victory, or to secure a retreat. The most decisive battles lose half their value to the conqueror, when the want of cavalry prevents him from following up his success, and depriving the enemy of the power of rallying.

When a retiring army is pursued, it is more especially upon the flanks that the weight of cavalry should fall, if you are strong enough in that arm to cut off his retreat.

## MAXIM LII

Artillery is more essential to cavalry than to infantry, because cavalry has no fire for its defence, but depends upon the sabre. It is to remedy this deficiency that recourse has been had to horse-artillery. Cavalry, therefore, should never be without cannon, whether when attacking, rallying, or in position.

NOTE.

Horse-artillery is an invention of Frederick. Austria lost no time in introducing it into her armies, although in an imperfect degree. It was only in 1792 that this arm was adopted in France, where it was brought rapidly to its present perfection.

The services of this arm during the wars of the Revolution were immense. It may be said to have changed to a certain extent the character of tactics, because its facility of movement enables it to bear with rapidity on every point where artillery can be employed with success. Napoleon has remarked in his memoirs that a flanking battery which strikes and rakes the enemy obliquely, is capable of deciding a victory in itself. To this we may add that, independent of the advantages which cavalry derives from horse-artillery in securing its flanks, and in opening the way for a successful charge by the destructiveness of its fire, it is desirable that these two arms should never be separated, but ready at all times to seize upon points where it may be necessary to employ cannon. On these occasions, the cavalry masks the march of the artillery, protects its establishment in position, and covers it from the attack of the enemy, until it is ready to open its fire.

## MAXIM LIII

In march, or in position, the greater part of the artillery should be with the divisions of infantry and cavalry. The rest should be in reserve. Each gun should have with it three hundred rounds, without including the limber. This is about the complement for two battles.

NOTE.

The better infantry is, the more important it is to support it by artillery, with a view to its preservation.

It is essential, also, that the batteries attached to divisions should march in the front, because this has a strong influence on the morale of the soldier. He attacks always with confidence when he sees the flanks of the column well covered with cannon.

The artillery reserve should be kept for a decisive moment, and then employed in full force, for it will be difficult for the enemy at such a time to presume to attack it.

There is scarcely an instance of a battery of sixty pieces of cannon having been carried by a charge of infantry or cavalry, unless where it was entirely without support, or in a position to be easily turned.

## MAXIM LIV

Artillery should always be placed in the most advantageous positions, and as far in front of the line of cavalry and infantry as possible, without compromising the safety of the guns.

Field batteries should command the whole country round from the level of the platform. They should on no account be masked on the right and left, but have free range in every direction.

NOTE.

The battery of eighteen pieces of cannon, which covered the centre of the Russian army at the battle of La Moskwa (Borodino), may be cited as an example.

Its position, upon a circular height which commanded the field in every direction, added so powerfully to its effect, that its fire alone sufficed, for a considerable time, to paralyze the vigorous attack made by the French with their right. Although twice broken, the left of the Russian army closed to this battery, as to a pivot, and twice recovered its former position. After repeated attacks, conducted with a rare intrepidity, the battery was at length carried by the French, but not till they had lost the élite of their army, and with it the Generals Caulincourt and Montbrun. Its capture decided the retreat of the Russian left.

I might advert likewise to another instance, in the campaign of 1809, and to the terrible effect produced by the hundred pieces of cannon of the Guard which General Lauriston directed, at the battle of Wagram, against the right of the Austrian army.

## MAXIM LV

A General should never put his army into cantonments, when he has the means of collecting supplies of forage and provisions, and of thus providing for the wants of the soldier in the field.

NOTE.

One great advantage which results from having an army in camp is, that it is easier to direct its spirit and maintain its discipline there. The soldier in cantonments abandons himself to repose; he ends by finding a pleasure in idleness, and in fearing to return to the field. The reverse takes place in a camp. There, a feeling of ennui, and a severer discipline, make him anxious for the opening of the campaign, to interrupt the monotony of the service and relieve it with the chances and variety of war. Besides, an army in camp is much more secure from a surprise than in cantonments—the defect of which usually consists in their occupying too great an extent of ground. When an army is obliged to go into quarters, the Marquis de Feuquière recommends a camp to be selected in front of the line, where the troops can be frequently assembled—sometimes suddenly, in order to exercise their vigilance, or for the sole purpose of bringing the different corps together.

## MAXIM LVI

A good general, a well-organized system, good instructions, and severe discipline, aided by effective establishments, will always make good troops, independently of the cause for which they fight.

At the same time, a love of country, a spirit of enthusiasm, a sense of national honor, and fanaticism, will operate upon young soldiers with advantage.

NOTE.

This remark appears to me less applicable to officers than to soldiers, for as war is not a state of things natural to man, it follows that those who maintain its cause must be governed by some strong excitement. Much enthusiasm and devotedness are required on the part of the troops for the general who commands, to induce an army to perform great actions in a war in which it takes no interest. This is sufficiently proved by the apathy of auxiliaries, unless when inspired by the conduct of their chief.

## MAXIM LVII

When a nation is without establishments and a military system, it is very difficult to organize an army.

NOTE.

This is an unanswerable truth, more particularly with reference to an army intended to act upon the system of modern war, and in which order, precision, and rapidity of movement, are the principal essentials to success.

## MAXIM LVIII

The first qualification of a soldier is fortitude under fatigue and privation. Courage is only the second; hardship, poverty and want, are the best school for a soldier.

NOTE.

Valor belongs to the young soldier as well as to the veteran; but in the former it is more evanescent. It is only by habits of service, and after several campaigns, that the soldier acquires that moral courage which makes him support the fatigues and privations of war without a murmur. Experience by this time has instructed him to supply his own wants. He is satisfied with what he can procure, because he knows that success is only to be obtained by fortitude and perseverance. Well might Napoleon say that misery and want were the best school for a soldier; for as nothing could be compared with the total destitution of the army of the Alps, when he assumed the command, so nothing could equal the brilliant success which he obtained with this army in the first campaign in Italy. The conquerors of Montenotte, Lodi, Castiglione, Bassano, Arcole and Rivoli had beheld, only a few months before, whole battalions covered with rags, and deserting for the want of subsistence.

## MAXIM LIX

There are five things the soldier should never be without—his musket, his ammunition, his knapsack, his provisions (for at least four days), and his entrenching-tool. The knapsack may be reduced to the smallest size possible, if it be thought proper, but the soldier should always have it with him.

NOTE.

It is fortunate that Napoleon has recognized the advantage of giving to every soldier an entrenching-tool. His authority is the best answer to the ridicule which has been thrown upon those who proposed it. An axe will be found to inconvenience the foot-soldier as little as the sword he wears at his side, and it will be infinitely more useful. When axes are given out to companies, or are carried by fatigue-men during a campaign, they are soon lost; and it often happens, when a camp is to be formed, that a difficulty arises in cutting wood and building huts for the soldier; whereas, by making the axe a part of every man's appointments, he is obliged to have it always with him; and whether the object be to entrench himself in a village, or to erect huts in a camp, the commander of a corps will speedily see the advantage of this innovation.

When once the axe has been generally adopted, we shall, perhaps, see the desirability of issuing pickaxes and shovels to particular companies, and also the benefit of more frequent entrenchments. It is more particularly during retreats that it is important to entrench when the army has reached a good position; for an entrenched camp not only furnishes the means of rallying troops which are pursued, but if it be fortified in such a manner as to render the issue of an attack doubtful to the enemy, it will not only sustain the morale of the soldier in the retreat, but afford the general-in-chief opportunities for resuming the offensive, and profiting by the first false movement on the part of his adversary. It will be recollected how Frederick, in the campaign of 1761, when surrounded by two Russian and Austrian armies, whose united force was quadruple his own, saved his army by entrenching himself in the camp of Buntzalvitz.

## MAXIM LX

Every means should be taken to attach the soldier to his colors. This is best accomplished by showing consideration and respect to the old soldier. His pay likewise should increase with his length of service. It is the height of injustice not to pay a veteran more than a recruit.

NOTE.

Some modern writers have recommended, on the other hand, to limit the period of service, in order to bring the whole youth of a country successively under arms. By this means they purpose to have the levies, en masse, all ready trained and capable of resisting successfully a war of invasion. But however advantageous at first sight such a military system may appear, I believe it will be found to have many objections.

In the first place, the soldier fatigued with the minutiæ of discipline in a garrison, will not feel much inclined to re-enlist after he has received his discharge, more especially since, having served the prescribed time, he will consider himself to have fulfilled all the duties of a citizen to his country. Returning to his friends, he will probably marry, or establish himself in a trade. From that moment his military spirit declines, and he soon becomes ill adapted to the business of war. On the contrary, the soldier who serves long, becomes attached to his regiment as to a new family. He submits to the yoke of discipline, accustoms himself to the privations his situation imposes, and ends by finding his condition agreeable. There are few officers that have seen service who have not discovered the difference between old and young soldiers, with reference to their power of supporting the fatigues of a long campaign, to the determined courage that characterizes the attack, or to the ease with which they rally after being broken.

Montécuculli observes, that "it takes time to discipline an army; more to inure it to war; and still more to constitute veterans." For this reason, he recommends that great consideration should be shown to old soldiers; that they should be carefully provided for, and a large body of them kept always on foot. It seems to me, also, that it is not enough to increase the pay of the soldier according to his period of service, but that it is highly essential to confer on him some mark of distinction that shall secure to him privileges calculated to encourage him to grow gray under arms, and, above all, to do so with honor.

## MAXIM LXI

It is not set speeches at the moment of battle that render soldiers brave. The veteran scarcely listens to them, and the recruit forgets them at the first discharge. If discourses and harangues are useful, it is during the campaign: to do away unfavorable impressions, to correct false reports, to keep alive a proper spirit in the camp, and to furnish materials and amusement for the bivouac. All printed orders of the day should keep in view these objects.

NOTE.

The opinion of the general-in-chief, energetically expressed, is, notwithstanding, productive of great effect on the morale of the soldier.

In 1703, at the attack of Hornbec, Marshal Villars, seeing the troops advancing without spirit, threw himself at their head: "What!" said he, "is it expected that I, a marshal of France, should be the first to escalade, when I order YOU to attack?"

These few words rekindled their ardor; officers and soldiers rushed upon the works, and the town was taken almost without loss.

"We have retired far enough for to-day; you know I always sleep upon the field of battle!" said Napoleon, as he flew through the ranks at the moment of resuming the offensive at Marengo. These few words sufficed to revive the courage of the soldiers, and to make them forget the fatigues of the day, during which almost every man had been engaged.

## MAXIM LXII

Tents are unfavorable to health. The soldier is best when he bivouacs, because he sleeps with his feet to the fire, which speedily dries the ground on which he lies. A few planks, or a little straw, shelter him from the wind.

On the other hand, tents are necessary for the superior officers, who have to write and to consult their maps. Tents should, therefore, be issued to these, with directions to them never to sleep in a house. Tents are always objects of observation to the enemy's staff. They afford information in regard to your numbers and the ground you occupy; while an army bivouacking in two or three lines, is only distinguishable from afar by the smoke which mingles with the clouds. It is impossible to count the number of the fires.

NOTE.

The acknowledged advantage of bivouacking is another reason for adding an entrenching-tool to the equipment of the soldier; for, with the assistance of the axe and shovel, he can hut himself without difficulty. I have seen huts erected with the branches of trees, covered with turf, where the soldier was perfectly sheltered from the cold and wet, even in the worst season.

## MAXIM LXIII

All information obtained from prisoners should be received with caution, and estimated at its real value. A soldier seldom sees anything beyond his company; and an officer can afford intelligence of little more than the position and movements of the division to which his regiment belongs. On this account, the general of an army should never depend upon the information derived from prisoners, unless it agrees with the reports received from the advanced guards, in reference to the position, etc., of the enemy.

NOTE.

Montécuculli wisely observes that "prisoners should be interrogated separately, in order to ascertain, by the agreement in their answers, how far they may be endeavoring to mislead you." Generally speaking, the information required from officers who are prisoners, should have reference to the strength and resources of the enemy, and sometimes to his localities and position. Frederick recommends that prisoners should be menaced with instant death if they are found attempting to deceive by false reports.

## MAXIM LXIV

Nothing is so important in war as an undivided command; for this reason, when war is carried on against a single power, there should be only one army, acting upon one base, and conducted by one chief.

NOTE.

"Success," says the Archduke Charles, "is only to be obtained by simultaneous efforts, directed upon a given point, sustained with constancy, and executed with decision." It rarely happens that any number of men who desire the same object are perfectly agreed as to the means of attaining it; and if the will of one individual is not allowed to predominate, there can be no ensemble in the execution of their operations; neither will they attain the end proposed. It is useless to confirm this maxim by examples. History abounds in them.

Prince Eugene and Marlborough would never have been so successful in the campaigns which they directed in concert, if a spirit of intrigue and difference of opinion had not constantly disorganized the armies opposed to them.

## MAXIM LXV

The same consequences which have uniformly attended long discussions and councils of war, will follow at all times. They will terminate in the adoption of the worst course, which in war is always the most timid, or, if you will, the most prudent. The only true wisdom in a general is determined courage.

NOTE.

Prince Eugene used to say that councils of war "are only useful when you want an excuse for attempting nothing." This was also the opinion of Villars. A general-in-chief should avoid, therefore, assembling a council on occasions of difficulty, and should confine himself to consulting separately his most experienced generals in order to benefit by their advice, while he is governed at the same time in his decision by his own judgment. By this means, he becomes responsible, it is true, for the measures he pursues; but he has the advantage also of acting upon his own conviction, and of being certain that the secret of his operations will not be divulged, as is usually the case where it is discussed by a council of war.

## MAXIM LXVI

In war, the general alone can judge of certain arrangements. It depends on him alone to conquer difficulties by his own superior talents and resolution.

NOTE.

The officer who obeys, whatever may be the nature or extent of his command, will always stand excused for executing implicitly the orders which have been given to him. This is not the case with the general-in-chief, on whom the safety of the army and the success of the campaign depend. Occupied, without intermission, in the whole process of observation and reflection, it is easy to conceive that he will acquire by degrees a solidity of judgment which will enable him to see things in a clearer and more enlarged point of view than his inferior generals.

Marshal Villars, in his campaigns, acted almost always in opposition to the advice of his generals, and he was almost always fortunate. So true it is, that a general, who feels confident in his talent for command, must follow the dictates of his own genius if he wishes to achieve success.

## MAXIM LXVII

To authorize generals or other officers to lay down their arms in virtue of a particular capitulation, under any other circumstances than when they are composing the garrison of a fortress, affords a dangerous latitude. It is destructive of all military character in a nation to open such a door to the cowardly, the weak, or even to the misdirected brave. Great extremities require extraordinary resolution. The more obstinate the resistance of an army, the greater the chances of assistance or of success.

How many seeming impossibilities have been accomplished by men whose only resource was death!

NOTE.

In the campaign of 1759, Frederick directed General Fink, with eighteen thousand men, upon Maxen, for the purpose of cutting off the Austrian army from the defiles of Bohemia. Surrounded by twice his numbers, Fink capitulated after a sharp action, and fourteen thousand men laid down their arms. This conduct was the more disgraceful, because General Winch, who commanded the cavalry, cut his way through the enemy. The whole blame of the surrender fell, therefore, upon Fink, who was tried afterward by a court-martial, and sentenced to be cashiered and imprisoned for two years.

In the campaign of Italy in 1796, the Austrian General Provéra capitulated with two thousand men in the castle of Cossaria. Subsequently, at the battle of La Favorite, the same general capitulated with a corps of six thousand men. I scarcely dare to revert to the shameful defection of General Mack in the capitulation of Ulm in 1805, where thirty thousand Austrians laid down their arms—when we have seen, during the wars of the Revolution, so many generals open themselves a way by a vigorous effort through the enemy, supported only by a few battalions.

## MAXIM LXVIII

There is no security for any sovereign, for any nation, or for any general, if officers are permitted to capitulate in the open field, and to lay down their arms in virtue of conditions favorable to the contracting party, but contrary to the interests of the army at large. To withdraw from danger, and thereby to involve their comrades in greater peril, is the height of cowardice. Such conduct should be proscribed, declared infamous, and made punishable with death. All generals, officers and soldiers, who capitulate in battle to save their own lives, should be decimated.

He who gives the order, and those who obey, are alike traitors, and deserve capital punishment.

NOTE.

Soldiers, who are almost always ignorant of the designs of their chief, cannot be responsible for his conduct. If he orders them to lay down their arms, they must do so; otherwise they fail in that law of discipline which is more essential to an army than thousands of men. It appears to me, therefore, under these circumstances, that the chiefs alone are responsible, and liable to the punishment due to their cowardice. We have no example of soldiers being wanting in their duty in the most desperate situations, where they are commanded by officers of approved resolution.

## MAXIM LXIX

There is but one honorable mode of becoming prisoner of war. That is, by being taken separately; by which is meant, by being cut off entirely, and when we can no longer make use of our arms. In this case, there can be no conditions, for honor can impose none. We yield to an irresistible necessity.

NOTE.

There is always time enough to surrender prisoner of war. This should be deferred, therefore, till the last extremity. And here I may be permitted to cite an example of rare obstinacy in defence, which has been related to me by ocular witnesses. The captain of grenadiers, Dubrenil, of the thirty-seventh regiment of the line, having been sent on detachment with his company, was stopped on the march by a large party of Cossacks, who surrounded him on every side. Dubrenil formed his little force into square, and endeavored to gain the skirts of a wood (within a few muskets' shot of the spot where he had been attacked), and reached it with very little loss. But as soon as the grenadiers saw this refuge secured to them, they broke and fled, leaving their captain and a few brave men, who were resolved not to abandon him, at the mercy of the enemy. In the meantime, the fugitives, who had rallied in the depth of the wood, ashamed of having forsaken their leader, came to the resolution of rescuing him from the enemy, if a prisoner, or of carrying off his body if he had fallen. With this view, they formed once more upon the outskirts, and opening a passage with their bayonets through the cavalry, penetrated to their captain, who, notwithstanding seventeen wounds, was defending himself still. They immediately surrounded him, and regained the wood with little loss. Such examples are not rare in the wars of the Revolution, and it were desirable to see them collected by some contemporary, that soldiers might learn how much is to be achieved in war by determined energy and sustained resolution.

## MAXIM LXX

The conduct of a general in a conquered country is full of difficulties. If severe, he irritates and increases the number of his enemies. If lenient, he gives birth to expectations which only render the abuses and vexations, inseparable from war, the more intolerable. A victorious general must know how to employ severity, justice and mildness by turns, if he would allay sedition or prevent it.

NOTE.

Among the Romans, generals were only permitted to arrive at the command of armies after having exercised the different functions of the magistracy. Thus by a previous knowledge of administration, they were prepared to govern the conquered provinces with all that discretion which a newly-acquired power, supported by arbitrary force, demands.

In the military institutions of modern times, the generals, instructed only in what concerns the operation of strategy and tactics, are obliged to intrust the civil departments of the war to inferior agents, who, without belonging to the army, render all those abuses and vexations, inseparable from its operations, still more intolerable.

This observation, which I do little more than repeat, seems to me, notwithstanding, deserving of particular attention; for if the leisure of general officers was directed in time of peace to the study of diplomacy—if they were employed in the different embassies which sovereigns send to foreign courts—they would acquire a knowledge of the laws and of the government of these countries, in which they may be called hereafter to carry on the war. They would learn also to distinguish those points of interest on which all treaties must be based, which have for their object the advantageous termination of a campaign. By the aid of this information they would obtain certain and positive results, since all the springs of action, as well as the machinery of war, would be in their hands. We have seen Prince Eugene, and Marshal Villars, each fulfilling with equal ability the duties of a general and a negotiator.

When an army which occupies a conquered province observes strict discipline, there are few examples of insurrection among the people, unless indeed resistance is provoked (as but too often happens), by the exactions of inferior agents employed in the civil administration.

It is to this point, therefore, that the general-in-chief should principally direct his attention, in order that the contributions imposed by the wants of the army may be levied with impartiality; and above all, that they may be applied to their true object, instead of serving to enrich the collectors, as is ordinarily the case.

## MAXIM LXXI

Nothing can excuse a general who takes advantage of the knowledge acquired in the service of his country, to deliver up her frontier and her towns to foreigners. This is a crime reprobated by every principle of religion, morality and honor.

NOTE.

Ambitious men who, listening only to their passions, arm natives of the same land against each other (under the deceitful pretext of the public good), are still more criminal. For however arbitrary a government, the institutions which have been consolidated by time, are always preferable to civil war, and to that anarchy which the latter is obliged to create for the justification of its crimes.

To be faithful to his sovereign, and to respect the established government, are the first principles which ought to distinguish a soldier and a man of honor.

## MAXIM LXXII

A general-in-chief has no right to shelter his mistakes in war under cover of his sovereign, or of a minister, when these are both distant from the scene of operation, and must consequently be either ill informed or wholly ignorant of the actual state of things.

Hence, it follows, that every general is culpable who undertakes the execution of a plan which he considers faulty. It is his duty to represent his reasons, to insist upon a change of plan, in short, to give in his resignation, rather than allow himself to be made the instrument of his army's ruin. Every general-in-chief who fights a battle in consequence of superior orders, with the certainty of losing it, is equally blamable.

In this last-mentioned case, the general ought to refuse obedience; because a blind obedience is due only to a military command given by a superior present on the spot at the moment of action. Being in possession of the real state of things, the superior has it then in his power to afford the necessary explanations to the person who executes his orders.

But supposing a general-in-chief to receive positive order from his sovereign, directing him to fight a battle, with the further injunction, to yield to his adversary, and allow himself to be defeated—ought he to obey it? No. If the general should be able to comprehend the meaning or utility of such an order, he should execute it; otherwise he should refuse to obey it.

NOTE.

In the campaign of 1697, Prince Eugene caused the courier to be intercepted, who was bringing him orders from the emperor forbidding him to hazard a battle, for which everything had been prepared, and which he foresaw would prove decisive. He considered, therefore, that he did his duty in evading the orders of his sovereign; and the victory of Zanta, in which the Turks lost about thirty thousand men, and four thousand prisoners, rewarded his audacity. In the meantime, notwithstanding the immense advantages which accrued from this victory to the imperial arms, Eugene was disgraced on his arrival at Vienna.

In 1793, General Hoche, having received orders to move upon Treves with an army harassed by constant marches in a mountainous and difficult country, refused to obey. He observed, with reason, that in order to obtain possession of an unimportant fortress, they were exposing his army to inevitable ruin. He caused, therefore, his troops to return into winter quarters, and preferred the preservation of his army, upon which the success of the future campaign depended, to his own safety. Recalled to Paris, he was thrown into a dungeon, which he only quitted on the downfall of Robespierre.

I dare not decide if such examples are to be imitated; but it seems to me highly desirable that a question so new and so important, should be discussed by men who are capable of determining its merits.

## MAXIM LXXIII

The first qualification in a general-in-chief is a cool head—that is, a head which receives just impressions, and estimates things and objects at their real value. He must not allow himself to be elated by good news, or depressed by bad.

The impressions he receives either successively or simultaneously in the course of the day, should be so classed as to take up only the exact place in his mind which they deserve to occupy; since it is upon a just comparison and consideration of the weight due to different impressions, that the power of reasoning and of right judgment depends.

Some men are so physically and morally constituted as to see everything through a highly-colored medium. They raise up a picture in the mind on every slight occasion, and give to every trivial occurrence a dramatic interest. But whatever knowledge, or talent, or courage, or other good qualities such men may possess, nature has not formed them for the command of armies, or the direction of great military operations.

NOTE.

"The first quality in a general-in-chief," says Montécuculli, "is a great knowledge of the art of war. This is not intuitive, but the result of experience. A man is not born a commander. He must become one. Not to be anxious; to be always cool; to avoid confusion in his commands; never to change countenance; to give his orders in the midst of battle with as much composure as if he were perfectly at ease. These are the proofs of valor in a general.

"To encourage the timid; to increase the number of the truly brave; to revive the drooping ardor of the troops in battle; to rally those who are broken; to bring back to the charge those who are repulsed; to find resources in difficulty, and success even amid disaster; to be ready at a moment to devote himself, if necessary, for the welfare of the state. These are the actions which acquire for a general distinction and renown."

To this enumeration may be added, the talent of discriminating character, and of employing every man in the particular post which nature has qualified him to fill. "My principal attention," said Marshal Villars, "was always directed to the study of the younger generals. Such a one I found, by the boldness of his character, fit to lead a column of attack; another, from a disposition naturally cautious, but without being deficient in courage, more perfectly to be relied on for the defence of a country." It is only by a just application of these personal qualities to their respective objects, that it is possible to command success in war.

## MAXIM LXXIV

The leading qualifications which should distinguish an officer selected for the head of the staff, are, to know the country thoroughly; to be able to conduct a reconnoissance with skill; to superintend the transmission of orders promptly; to lay down the most complicated movements intelligibly, but in a few words, and with simplicity.

NOTE.

Formerly, the duties of the chiefs of the staff were confined to the necessary preparations for carrying the plan of the campaign, and the operations resolved on by the general-in-chief, into effect. In a battle, they were only employed in directing movements and superintending their execution. But in the late wars, the officers of the staff were frequently intrusted with the command of a column of attack, or of large detachments, when the general-in-chief feared to disclose the secret of his plans by the transmission of orders or instructions. Great advantages have resulted from this innovation, although it was long resisted. By this means, the staff have been enabled to perfect their theory by practice, and they have acquired, moreover, the esteem of the soldiers and junior officers of the line, who are easily led to think lightly of their superiors, whom they do not see fighting in the ranks. The generals who have held the arduous situation of chief of the staff during the wars of the Revolution, have almost always been employed in the different branches of the profession. Marshal Berthier, who filled so conspicuously this appointment to Napoleon, was distinguished by all the essentials of a general. He possessed calm, and at the same time brilliant courage, excellent judgment, and approved experience. He bore arms during half a century, made war in the four quarters of the globe, opened and terminated thirty-two campaigns. In his youth he acquired, under the eye of his father, who was an engineer officer, the talent of tracing plans and finishing them with exactness, as well as the preliminary qualifications necessary to form a staff-officer. Admitted by the Prince de Lambesq into his regiment of dragoons, he was taught the skilful management of his horse and his sword—accomplishments so important to a soldier. Attached afterward to the staff of Count Rochambeau, he made his first campaign in America, where he soon began to distinguish himself by his valor, activity and talents. Having at length attained superior rank in the staff-corps formed by Marshal de Segur, he visited the camps of the King of Prussia, and discharged the duties of chief of the staff under the Baron de Bezenval.

During nineteen years, consumed in sixteen campaigns, the history of Marshal Berthier's life was little else but that of the wars of Napoleon, all the details of which he directed, both in the cabinet and the field. A stranger to the intrigues of politics, he labored with indefatigable activity; seized with promptitude and sagacity upon general views, and gave the necessary orders for attaining them with prudence, perspicuity, and conciseness. Discreet, impenetrable, modest; he was just, exact, and even severe, in everything that regarded the service; but he always set an example of vigilance and zeal in his own person, and knew how to maintain discipline, and to cause his authority to be respected by every rank under his orders.

## MAXIM LXXV

A commandant of artillery should understand well the general principles of each branch of the service, since he is called upon to supply arms and ammunition to the different corps of which it is composed. His correspondence with the commanding officers of artillery at the advanced posts, should put him in possession of all the movements of the army, and the disposition and management of the great park of artillery should depend upon this information.

NOTE.

After having recognized the advantage of intrusting the supply of arms and ammunition for an army to a military body, it appears to me extraordinary that the same regulation does not extend to that of provisions and forage, instead of leaving it in the hands of a separate administration, as is the practice at present.

The civil establishments attached to armies are formed almost always at the commencement of a war, and composed of persons strangers to those laws of discipline which they are but too much inclined to disregard. These men are little esteemed by the military, because they serve only to enrich themselves, without respect to the means. They consider only their private interest in a service whose glory they cannot share, although some portion of its success depends upon their zeal. The disorders and defalcations incident to these establishments would assuredly cease, if they were confided to men who had been employed in the army, and who, in return for their labors, were permitted to partake with their fellow-soldiers the triumph of their success.

## MAXIM LXXVI

The qualities which distinguish a good general of advanced posts, are, to reconnoitre accurately defiles and fords of every description; to provide guides that may be depended on; to interrogate the curé and postmaster; to establish rapidly a good understanding with the inhabitants; to send out spies; to intercept public and private letters; to translate and analyze their contents; in a word, to be able to answer every question of the general-in-chief, when he arrives with the whole army.

NOTE.

Foraging parties, composed of small detachments, and which were usually intrusted to young officers, served formerly to make good officers of advanced posts; but now the army is supplied with provisions by regular contributions: it is only in a course of partisan warfare that the necessary experience can be acquired to fill these situations with success.

A chief of partisans is, to a certain extent, independent of the army. He receives neither pay nor provisions from it, and rarely succor, and is abandoned during the whole campaign to his own resources.

An officer so circumstanced must unite address with courage, and boldness with discretion, if he wishes to collect plunder without measuring the strength of his little corps with superior forces. Always harassed, always surrounded by dangers, which it is his business to foresee and surmount, a leader of partisans acquires in a short time an experience in the details of war rarely to be obtained by an officer of the line; because the latter is almost always under the guidance of superior authority, which directs the whole of his movements, while the talent and genius of the partisan are developed and sustained by a dependence on his own resources.

## MAXIM LXXVII

Generals-in-chief must be guided by their own experience, or their genius. Tactics, evolutions, the duties and knowledge of an engineer or artillery officer, may be learned in treatises, but the science of strategy is only to be acquired by experience, and by studying the campaigns of all the great captains.

Gustavus Adolphus, Turenne, and Frederick, as well as Alexander, Hannibal, and Cæsar, have all acted upon the same principles. These have been: to keep their forces united; to leave no weak part unguarded; to seize with rapidity on important points.

Such are the principles which lead to victory, and which, by inspiring terror at the reputation of your arms, will at once maintain fidelity and secure subjection.

NOTE.

"A great captain can only be formed," says the Archduke Charles, "by long experience and intense study: neither is his own experience enough—for whose life is there sufficiently fruitful of events to render his knowledge universal?" It is, therefore, by augmenting his information from the stock of others, by appreciating justly the discoveries of his predecessors, and by taking for his standard of comparison those great military exploits, in connection with their political results, in which the history of war abounds, that he can alone become a great commander.

## MAXIM LXXVIII

Peruse again and again the campaigns of Alexander, Hannibal, Cæsar, Gustavus Adolphus, Turenne, Eugene, and Frederick. Model yourself upon them. This is the only means of becoming a great captain, and of acquiring the secret of the art of war. Your own genius will be enlightened and improved by this study, and you will learn to reject all maxims foreign to the principles of these great commanders.

NOTE.

It is in order to facilitate this object that I have formed the present collection. It is after reading and meditating upon the history of modern war that I have endeavored to illustrate, by examples, how the maxims of a great captain may be most successfully applied to this study. May the end I have had in view be accomplished!

www.ingramcontent.com/pod-product-compliance
Lightning Source LLC
LaVergne TN
LVHW090038080526
838202LV00046B/3870